IT'S A WRAP!

also by Andrew Laszlo

EVERY FRAME A REMBRANDT

FOOTNOTE TO HISTORY

THE SEVEN GRACES OF GOD

THE RAT CATCHER

IT'S A WRAP!

Andrew Laszlo, ASC

THE ASC PRESS
HOLLYWOOD, CALIFORNIA

First Published in 2004
10 9 8 7 6 5 4 3 2 1
Printed in the United States

Library of Congress Cataloging-in-Pubication Data
Laszlo, Andrew, author

It's A Wrap

1. Cinematography   2. Motion Pictures 3. Television

ISBN 0-935578-23-4

Copyright© 2004 by Andrew Laszlo, ASC
All Rights Reserved

ASC PRESS

The American Society of Cinematographers
1782 North Orange Drive
Hollywood, California, 90028

For information on all ASC Press
publications available go to www.theasc.com

Cover design by Marion Gore
Book design by Martha Winterhalter
Edited by Rachael Bosley

Printed in the United States by Paper Chase Printing

CONTENTS

INTRODUCTION

My interest in photography goes back to around 1932-33, when I was 7 years old. At that time, I watched with fascination as some of my older cousins made photographic prints of the pictures they had taken with their box cameras. After the negatives were developed, they were placed in a frame with light-sensitive paper and put out into sunlight for the positive image to transfer to paper. After several checks over a considerable time, when the print was thought to be the right density, it was removed from the frame and placed into a fixing solution to make it permanent.

This was my first exposure to the mysterious and magical world of photography — seeing the wonder of images captured by a camera brought to life by sunshine. The next turning point came when my brother gave me a camera he had received as a confirmation present, but didn't want. It was a neat little camera, a step above the box-Brownie variety; its front cover had to be opened and the bellows had to be carefully dragged forward on tracks until they clicked into place and the camera was ready to take pictures. That led to the next step in my involvement and education in photography: developing the film and enlarging the pictures. At that time, in the late 1930s, this was easier said than done.

I lived in a relatively small town in western Hungary called Pápa, and darkrooms equipped with enlargers and other equipment necessary to process pictures were mostly the domain of professional photographers. Equipment was expensive, and such necessities as ready-made developing and fixing solutions could not be bought. They didn't exist. Chemical components had to be purchased and the solutions had to be prepared by the user. This meant I had to find books on the chemistry aspects of photography, locate the manufacturers of the chemical components, and buy chemicals from sources that were sometimes outside of the country. Before I was ready to mix my first batch of developing solution, I had to assemble the lab equipment: scales, beakers and trays, and bottles to store the developer, stop bath and fixing solutions.

The biggest and most difficult piece of equipment to come by was an enlarger. There were a few sources in the country selling them at exorbitant prices I couldn't afford. The only way for me to have a fully equipped darkroom was to make all the necessary equipment myself. The first enlarger I made didn't work well. The second one surprised even me; it worked exceptionally well for the primitive device it was. The body was made from a section of an aluminum milk can. It contained the light source, two condenser lenses I was able to "liberate" from two identical flashlights, the film holder, and the bellows and a lens salvaged from an old camera. A contact printer, which by this time was using an electric light bulb instead of sunlight, and several developing, fixing and washing trays, all made of wood, rounded out the necessities of a workable darkroom. Now that I had the equipment, the next problem was that aside from the family bathroom, which was available only at night, I had no place to set it up.

But the wonders of seeing images appear slowly on the surfaces of blank sheets of photographic paper in the developing solutions; the mystique of working in dim, red light; and the smell of the chemicals, which I learned to love, more than compensated for the inconveniences of setting up my equipment after my family had gone to bed and staying up most of the night to do the work. Working in the darkroom got me deeply into photography. The more I experimented, the more I learned, and the more I learned, the more I wanted to know. Learning composition, working with light and experimenting with unusual techniques fanned the flames of my curiosity, and it all added up to a fairly high level of proficiency.

The next level of image creation, motion-picture photography, loomed over the horizon like a mirage, but in a small, middle European country, getting involved in filmmaking seemed impossible at that time. There were no schools teaching film production in Hungary or, as far as I knew, anywhere else in the world. And even if there were, I could not have attended them. The time period was the early 1940s, and World War II, which had been raging for some time by then, dashed any hope I had of getting even close to the film industry.

The war years had a devastating effect on my life. My entire family perished in the Holocaust. Having survived that terrible era of history, I returned to my hometown, and for some time supported myself by photographing Russian soldiers with recovered photo equipment that had been hidden for me by a friend.

In 1946, I was fortunate enough to land an apprentice position at one of the two motion-picture studios in Budapest, but film production in that war-torn country was at a virtual standstill. There was no way to satisfy my hunger for learning about and getting involved in film production, nor did the foreseeable future hold any promise that this would happen. With my family gone, I decided it was time to leave Hungary, and less than a year later I arrived in the United States as a Displaced Person, eager and full of high hopes and expectations. But life in the "Land of Plenty" turned out not to be as easy as I had hoped. My priorities were to keep my head above water and learn enough of the English language quickly so I could get work that was in some way connected with photography.

Working in the darkroom of a company that made textiles and wallpaper that were printed with a photographic process kept my fingers in developer and hypo, and later, door-to-door baby photography kept me current with cameras, film, exposure and the use of a minimal amount of lighting equipment. Then, in 1950, my big break came: I was drafted by the Army. I managed to wind up in the Signal Corps, and after completing the Army Motion Picture School, I wound up in a photographic unit that gave me unlimited opportunities to shoot miles and miles of 35mm motion-picture film and allowed me to gain experience and confidence.

I was married shortly before my discharge from the service in 1952. But getting my first civilian job was not easy. Though I thought of myself as an accomplished and talented cinematographer, trying to break into and get established in a relatively small industry, as even the American film industry was, was very difficult. The breaks came slowly, but fortunately, they did come, and before long I was working on better and better projects, mostly as a camera operator. Though I was marginally able to support my wife and one child, perseverance, connections and luck slowly paid off, and I was able to land some projects that were popular with the public and recognized by the industry as well.

My first mainstream job as a camera operator was on the hit CBS series *The Phil Silvers Show* (1953-1957). This was followed by a number of other well-known television shows. One of these was the very popular ABC series *Naked City* (1959-1963), which gave me the opportunity to move up to the director of photography position. In 1962, before the series went off the air, I was offered my first feature film, *One Potato, Two Potato*. This movie, which screened at the Cannes Film Festival, was highly controversial but a very successful and acclaimed film for the time. Thanks to the success and popularity of these projects, I spent the next three years filming some top television films, including *The Man Without a Country*, which brought me my first Emmy nomination in 1972. Some of these projects brought me in contact with personalities like Lillian Gish, Helen Hayes, Maureen O'Hara, Jean Simmons, Ray Milland, Robert Ryan, Cliff Robertson, Maurice Chevalier and many, many others.

Better and bigger feature films slowly preempted television work. Francis Ford Coppola's *You're A Big Boy Now* (1966), my second feature, was a huge success and was heralded by some critics for ushering in a new wave of film production and cinematography. *The Night They Raided Minsky's* (1968), a star-studded, big-budget musical directed by Billy Friedkin, was expected to be a smash hit, and it probably would have been, had it not been for the death of Bert Lahr, the film's lead, in the middle of production. In 1979, I briefly returned to television work with *Shōgun*, which brought me my second Emmy nomination.

More than 30 feature films filled the years between 1968 and 1991, when I retired from feature-film production upon completing *Newsies,* a large-scale musical for Walt Disney Pictures. The talents with whom I worked during those years are too numerous to list here, but mentioning some will suggest the caliber of people with whom I worked throughout my professional life: actors Jeff Bridges, Bill Cosby, Robert Duvall, Willem Dafoe, Ossie Davis, Joel Grey, John Huston, Diane Keaton, Jack Lemmon, Sophia Loren, Ann-Margret, Toshiro Mifune, Sidney Poitier, Meg Ryan, Jason Robards and Barbra Streisand; directors Coppola, Friedkin, Walter Hill, Arthur Hiller, Michael Powell, Guy Hamilton and Ted Kotcheff; and producers Jerry Bruckheimer, James Clavell, Michael Finnell, Frank Marshall, Steven Spielberg and Joel Silver.

But the most important people around me were my family: my wife, three sons and a beautiful daughter. As much as I liked the wonderful opportunities my work gave me to travel, the downside of the film profession was the time I had to spend away from my family. But some of the trips, particularly the ones on which my wife and children, could join me, were wonderful.

I have been fortunate enough to be invited into some of the prestigious organizations of the film world. I served two terms as a governor of the Academy of Television Arts and Sciences, and I am still an active member of the Academy of Motion Picture Arts and Sciences. In 2003, I received my Gold Membership Card for completing 50 years in the International Cinematographers Guild. Memberships in the Directors Guild of America and the very prestigious American Society of Cinematographers round out the list.

After retiring from feature-film production in 1991, I continued photographing top television commercials for several more years. I loved the challenges and opportunities these projects presented, but after another five years behind the camera, I decided the time had come to give something back. Since then, I have devoted my time to teaching film students and film professionals at home in the United States, as well as in many other countries. My first book, *Every Frame a Rembrandt,* is required reading in many university-level cinematography courses, and I hope it will be followed by others in the years to come. Writing has always been one of my favorite pastimes, and many of my technical articles have been published by leading industry publications around the world. Next to writing, I enjoy fly-fishing and wood- and metalworking, and I still spend many a day and night in my darkroom, working with a homemade enlarger and printer.

I look back over 50 years in the film industry with pride and satisfaction. I think of the projects I did and the people with whom I worked fondly, and I don't believe I have much to apologize for. I loved what I accomplished as a cinematographer, and it fills me with great pride to note that the selection committee of the Worldfest-Houston International Film & Video Festival thought enough of my accomplishments to honor me with a Lifetime Achievement Award in 2001.

FOREWORD

I believe the title of this book calls for an explanation. "It's a wrap" is not a totally unheard-of expression, but in the worldwide film industry, it has a very special application aside from its regular meaning and use. That application is what prompted me to write this book. Let me explain.

When "It's a wrap" is heard on a set, it is usually a much-welcomed announcement of the completion of work for the day. But when the same expression is heard unexpectedly, at times in the middle of the day, it usually has a very different connotation. At such times, "It's a wrap" might mean that something does not or will not work as planned; the work is stopped and can't be continued. For example, it's raining when sunshine is needed; somebody brought the wrong equipment for the shot; or the star and the director have had what the industry calls (snidely) "an artistic or creative difference of opinion," and one of them, or both, have walked off the set. It is very likely that when something like that happens, "It's a wrap" will be spoken quietly, most likely by a crewmember, and usually with deliberate understatement or pronounced sarcasm. This book concentrates on those occasions, as well as unexpected hitches that could not have been foreseen and avoided — incidents that stopped the work and prompted the cry or whisper "It's a wrap!"

With this out of the way, let me briefly tell you about myself and my work and introduce other elements of this book that may not have anything to do with planning or the lack of it, events that simply happened and affected the production or, in some ways, my life. My lifelong infatuation with the camera — I've spent well over 50 years looking through the viewfinder — has filled my life with the rewards and challenges of my craft and art, and with the indescribable joy of facing up to and conquering those challenges. Working on many feature films provided me with a privileged life that allowed me to visit some of the most beautiful and interesting corners of the world, and brought me in contact with the stars, directors, producers and personalities of the world of "make-believe." Likewise, documentary films helped me expand my horizons of the "real world," and sent me to the far corners of the planet to explore and film wonders and mysteries that few are fortunate enough to see and experience. Working in the film industry allowed me to look into the lives of the wealthy, the famous and the unfortunate, and even visit and live amongst some of the still-remaining Stone Age tribes of South America. It put me alongside explorers, scientists, presidents and kings, top athletes, and high achievers in the world of business, as well as card sharks and drug addicts, an unbelievable cross-section of the world's population that most people only read about.

But it was the day-to-day activities of the motion-picture business that provided me with fulfillment — or caused high anxiety — as I did my work on the sets and back lots of Hollywood and at real locations around the world. Dealing with the responsibilities of committing the writer's imagination and the director's vision to film, helping others with their jobs, and dealing with studio politics and the egos of some stars and personalities made my life interesting, to say the least. But the intensity of the work also allowed some light moments to creep in between the extreme pressures for which the film industry is known; moments of pent-up tensions erupting into uncontrollable laughter were like rays of sunshine peeking around the golden edge of storm clouds. Most of these moments were spontaneous, unexpected, welcome or devastating: as they either created incredible tension or released the pressures and anxieties of the work with lighthearted fun.

One of these light moments still brings a smile to my face, though I no longer remember what movie or television show I was working on when it happened. The scene was routine and simple, one I had done many times before and have done many times since in a number of films and television shows, a scene some of us in the business refer to simply (or snidely) as a "standard morgue scene." Picture a couple of detectives bringing a sobbing person in to identify a corpse under a sheet on the slab in the morgue. The sheet is lifted, the sobbing person breaks down, and the detectives exchange knowing looks. That's how I remember the scene as my camera was in position. The table was in the foreground and the cast was waiting to come in through the door at the far wall of the set. The whole scene was to be one shot.

We were ready to film when it was discovered that we had no corpse. As the corpse was not going to be seen, some penny-pinching accountant in the production office might have figured "if you don't see it, you don't need it." But we did need a body under the sheet. The director was impatient to get going, not wanting to waste valuable production time with such a routine shot, and he told an assistant to grab an extra, any extra, and put him or her under the sheet. The assistant director picked a young woman who might have had a fleeting moment of hope of being discovered, getting a big break in show biz, particularly because she was told that she would get extra pay to play a corpse.

It wasn't very obvious until the sheet was draped over her that she was an extremely well-endowed young lady. Much to the amusement and delight of the crew, her large breasts formed a well-defined mound under the sheet. There were a few snickers and some quiet wisecracks but, of course, the "corpse," the young woman, had no idea about what was going on because she was under the sheet and couldn't see. The actors — white-coated morgue attendants, the detectives and the mourner — were standing by, waiting for the cue to enter the set and play their parts. The nervous director was yelling, "Let's go! Let's get going!" and the assistant director called for quiet and the camera to roll. All were waiting for the director to call "Action," but instead, our nervous director, seeing the large mound under the sheet, must have thought that the "corpse" had her arms crossed. He jumped in front of the camera, pushed down on the extra's breasts with both hands and yelled, "Put your hands down, honey, put your hands down!" The poor girl, lying blind under the sheet, had no idea who was grabbing her breasts or why, but the shock of being grabbed so unexpectedly and with such force just about made her take off like a rocket. She tried desperately to get out from under the sheet and struggled to get off the table, but the harder she tried, the harder the director pushed her down. Most on the set thought this was funny, except for the poor young woman, who, with her hopes of stardom dashed, ran off the set crying. She was promptly replaced with a beat-up, taped-together dummy that had survived countless falls, having been thrown off rooftops and bridges whenever a body was seen falling in a show.

We were ready to roll again. The director called "Action," the detectives and the mourner came into the room, but as the sheet was lifted, instead of breaking down in deep sorrow, our mourner, seeing the oversized, moth-eaten, beat-up rag doll with stuffing coming out of its hip and elbows, broke up in uncontrollable laughter, and we had to cut the camera. Take two. I knew from past experience that even before the sheet was lifted, our actress would break up again. She did, but I left the camera running for some time before I cut. The third time around, as the detectives and the mourner approached the marble slab, all broke up before they even got to the table. The reactions to the first two takes, suppressed snickers, grew into an uncontrollable laughing fit as the entire cast and crew broke up, and it became obvious that we could not even attempt a fourth take. The only person who wasn't laughing was our director, who walked off the set in total frustration.

If nothing else, I knew we had a wonderful gem for the "gag reel" that would be shown at the next Christmas party. It was quite obvious to all that no amount of magic could stem the tide of laughter and, being late in the afternoon, it was a wrap for the day.

A couple of days later, before we attempted to shoot the same scene again, an announcement was made that any actor or crewmember who laughed would be instantly fired. Oddly enough, when we shot the scene, nobody even smiled — not because of the threat of being dismissed, but because the spontaneous, contagious set hysteria was not there. The routine, close-to-boring shot was made in one or two takes.

Incidents such as this can be very funny, and you have probably seen more than a few in various blooper reels on television. But it is not my intention to focus on such bloopers. Instead, I intend to concentrate on unusual, unexpected and interesting events and incidents that influenced and affected a particular project I was working on, as well as my life, during half a century in the fast lane of filmmaking.

KIDNAPPED

We had been flying for some time. I had just finished a sumptuous meal in the first-class cabin when Ed Sullivan asked my assistant to change seats with him and sat down next to me. "Andriu." He turned to me with a very serious expression. "I lied to you." This was a very unexpected and, I might add, strange thing to say, and I didn't know what to make of it. Ed was a fine and very reserved gentleman. I never knew him to kid around, and at that moment, as ever, his expression was serious. But it was never easy to gauge Ed by his expression. Many referred to him as "Mr. Deadpan," and some even claimed that Ed had only two expressions: one with and one without his hat. (Incidentally, I'd never seen Ed wear a hat.) I wondered what he was leading up to, what it was he had lied to me about. I figured it had something to do with the course of the last three days, and thoughts raced through my head as I tried to come up with a clue to help me understand his statement: "Andriu, I lied to you."

I came to be on the plane with Ed Sullivan because of a phone call the previous Sunday afternoon. I recognized the familiar, friendly voice. "Hello, Andy, this is Clay Adams. I hope I didn't wake you," he said cheerfully, knowing full well that on Sundays I sometimes took a nap in the afternoon. But it was always a pleasure to hear from Clay. As was his custom, he came directly to the point. He was one of the top producers at CBS, and as such, calling people on Sundays or waking them up at any hour of the day or night never seemed to bother him.

Some of my friends swear that producers or production managers are totally lacking in sensitivity and consideration and have no heart. One friend insists that if he ever needed a heart transplant, he would try to get a producer's heart, because according to him, no producer's heart has ever been used. But I don't agree, certainly not as it involves Clay, who by that time was not only my boss, but also a very good friend and the godfather of my youngest son. He was, perhaps, best known in the business as the director of the award-winning TV series *Victory at Sea*.

I woke fully as Clay got into what he was calling about, which sounded interesting and exciting; besides, it was business, and that was always welcome. First he had me promise that everything he was about to tell me would be kept in strict confidence, and no mention of anything about this assignment would be disclosed outside of my immediate family. My ears perked up as he gave me the details. Ed Sullivan, he explained, was going to have a private interview with President Trujillo of the Dominican Republic. He explained further that Ed had personally asked that I photograph the interview. I knew this was a compliment, which I appreciated. The prospect of going to the Dominican Republic also sounded exciting. I'd been there before and liked the place, but best of all, I considered myself fortunate to work with Ed Sullivan again. By that time, I'd done several very interesting projects with him and knew he liked me. I was also very fond of him, and I told Clay I would be delighted to do the project.

Clay explained that Ed wanted to leave for Ciudad Trujillo, then the capital of the Dominican Republic (named after El Presidente), on Wednesday; film the interview on Thursday; return to New York on Friday; edit the footage on Saturday and air the exclusive interview on his Sunday night show. It sounded like a piece of cake. The filming was to take place in the presidential palace, and because of the confidential nature of the interview, the crew, Clay suggested, should be kept to a minimum. No family members would be permitted to come along, and Clay thought I should carry no more equipment than was absolutely necessary. I agreed that Monday and Tuesday would give me sufficient time to put a crew and the necessary equipment together in order to leave on Wednesday. Clay promised to give me the details about flights, hotels and so on by Tuesday evening.

The job promised to be a plum. It was the kind of assignment one can neither find in the job listings of any newspaper, nor apply for if and when it is rumored to happen. It was the kind of job I and my contemporaries in the film and television industry dream about and hope to get. In the freelance-oriented film and television business, steady employment is rare, and a job such as mine at that time, working on a successful television series, the very popular *Phil Silvers Show*, and getting a paycheck every week was wonderful. But a plum like this, out of the blue, was a welcome change of pace, especially while my regular show was on hiatus. It meant first-class travel, living high on the hog and collecting per diem, which usually amounted to several months' worth of pocket money. This job had the promise of a godsend.

As good as it was working on *The Phil Silvers Show*, after a while even it became a bit repetitious and monotonous. Now, here I was, on a quiet Sunday afternoon, asked to put this job together and go spend a couple of days in the Dominican Republic. It was going to be a pleasure and a piece of cake! Maybe two or three hours of work, then the pool-side bar and a tall Piña Colada or Rum Collins made with real, dark and fragrant Planters Rum. Life was beautiful, and I was fortunate to be in a great business, working steadily on a hit show for a big company like CBS and, when the show stopped for hiatus, occasionally working on such other programs as *The Ed Sullivan Show*.

By that time, *The Ed Sullivan Show* was the number one show on U.S. television. It had the highest ratings of any TV show, which was interesting because some critics considered Ed to be totally without talent. They said he couldn't act, dance or sing and, more often than not, they claimed he even had a problem remembering his lines, in spite of cue cards. Yet, at 8 o'clock every Sunday night, the country came to a standstill as everyone tuned in *The Ed Sullivan Show*. I was fortunate to work on that show occasionally, and the biggest bonus was working in very close proximity to Ed, whom I knew well enough by that time to be on a first-name basis with.

Ed started out as a newspaper columnist, covering the entertainment world in Hollywood and New York, and that's how, as I understand it, he more or less fell into the slot of becoming the master of ceremonies on a show of variety acts. Before long, he was hosting the top entertainers of the world: actors, singers, dancers, magicians and acrobats, and the popularity of his show skyrocketed. The best performing talents would have given anything for a chance to be on *The Ed Sullivan Show*. It was said that being on the show meant immediate fame and fortune, which in many cases was true. When The Beatles gave their very first large concert — the granddaddy of all rock concerts, which I was fortunate to photograph in New York at Shea Stadium — they were paid the until-then-unheard-of fee of $1.6 million. Three months later, they appeared on *The Ed Sullivan Show* (for the last of their three contracted appearances) for what was rumored to be less than $2,000.

There was a golf tournament on the TV that I didn't tune in or have any interest in, but which must have come on while I was dozing. I turned it off and went to work. I had two days to put this gig together and wanted to waste no time. Moments after I finished talking with Clay, I picked up the phone again.

The first and most important person I had to get was a top first assistant cameraman. My choice was Manny Alpert, who had worked with me on several projects in the past and was a friend going back to our Army days, the two of us having served in the same unit in the Signal Corps. Because it was Sunday, Manny was also at home, and he didn't mind me calling him on the weekend any more than I minded Clay calling me. Fortunately, he was available and agreed to do the job with me. We worked out the equipment list, ready to be ordered and checked out the following morning. Clay told me he had already contacted Ernie Zatorsky, a very fine sound engineer who also had worked with me on a number of shows. Ernie was going to bring his own equipment, Clay told me. Clay also suggested that I go easy on the lights, take a few easily transportable, lightweight units, just enough to light two people as they sat and talked. He thought that if I needed additional lights, they would be available locally. This was good advice, because when I had worked overseas in the past, there were always problems with incompatible plugs, different electrical standards of voltage and wiring, and I generally ended up using local equipment.

I was in town early Monday morning, checking out the equipment with Manny. I selected a Mitchell BNC camera, the finest sound camera at the time, and was careful to make sure that it was equipped to operate on 110 volts of electricity. In a studio environment, the cameras generally ran on 220 volts, but I didn't think the presidential palace in the Dominican Republic would have 220-volt outlets, so I opted for a 110-volt motor on the camera. Likewise, the lighting units I selected were three "Colortran" kits, consisting of three lights per large, suitcase-sized case. These were a relatively new type of light at that time, and though they were not used in studio photography, they were very popular with documentary and commercial filmmakers who liked to travel light and move fast on the job. They had many very handy aspects, two of which were that they could be plugged into regular household outlets, and their intensity could be adjusted by a small step-up transformer. Their color temperature at the highest setting was correct for color photography. The units used standard light bulbs, the most popular of which was the 150-watt, mushroom-shaped bulb used in homes in "high hat"-type ceiling units.

One item I never had enough of on overseas assignments was extension cords. I had discovered some time before this job that electric outlets were not as easily found overseas as they were in American buildings. So I took lots of heavy-duty extension cords and a bunch of Cube Taps, the kind of dividers one plugs into the end of an extension cord to create three outlets. A dozen spare bulbs rounded out our electric equipment. By the end of the day, Manny and I were satisfied that we had all the bases covered, and on Wednesday morning, Manny and a CBS driver were going to pick up the equipment. All we had to do now was go home, pack our personal things the following day and meet at the airport Wednesday morning.

These were the assignments I truly loved — first-class travel; accommodations in the best hotels; eating in the best restaurants; VIP status; exciting, expensive locations the average person can only dream about, and, best of all, all of it at someone else's expense.

Clay called again on Tuesday evening. He already knew the equipment had been taken care of, and that I had enough film for five interviews, but he wanted to let me know that I wouldn't have to check in at the airline counter. A CBS contact man was going to check all of us in in advance and take care of the luggage, so I should go directly to the VIP lounge.

I did just that the following morning. The CBS contact introduced me to some airline executives, all of who were eagerly waiting to meet Ed Sullivan. But Ed was late — not so late as to miss the flight, but not early enough for idle conversations. When he did arrive, there was just enough time to shake hands all the way around and head for the plane. We were the last to board. As soon as we got aboard and took our seats in the first-class compartment, the doors of the plane closed and we taxied away from the ramp.

The plane — a DC-4, maybe a DC-6 or a Lockheed Constellation, I really don't remember which — was luxurious, big and new for the time. It had four engines, propellers of course, and, as air travel of the day dictated, the food in the first-class compartment on long trips was outstanding. Champagne, the best wines and drinks of all kind flowed freely, and most of the food was prepared on board and served on fine china on a starched-cloth-covered tray. When lunch was over and the dishes were cleared away, just as I reached for a cigarette, Ed came over and asked Manny, who was sitting with me, to change seats with him. Of course, Manny obliged, and Ed sat down next to me. He had a glass of milk in hand. "Andriu" — a name he had called me for some time by then — "I lied to you."

He sipped his milk and let me hang. I actually liked the name "Andriu." A memory of some years before drifted back. We were sitting around a very large table in the dining room of the Gresham Hotel on O'Connell Street in Dublin. We had just arrived from Portugal, there was no work scheduled for the first evening, and the entire crew congregated for dinner. Ed, as usual, was the last to arrive, and he sat down next to me at the end of the table. The waiter was already taking orders, which took some time because there were many of us, and everybody had some special request, question or instruction about the food. Some wanted their steaks just so; others wanted to know if the shrimp was fresh, or if chips were the same as French fries — some pretty ludicrous questions, wasting time. But these were the pleasures of overseas assignments, living high on the hog and asserting one's self-importance in a way that at home just would not have been possible. As film crews, we thought of ourselves as special people deserving of special treatment.

I could sense Ed's growing impatience with and dislike for the posturing and suspected that he was also annoyed by not getting his due from the waiter, who had no clue as to who or how important Ed Sullivan was. All in all, by the time the waiter got to our end of the table, I was also pretty tired of and embarrassed by all the self-indulgent hot air, and when the waiter finally got to me, I simply asked for a grilled-cheese sandwich. Ed grabbed my arm. "Andy…rew," he stuttered, obviously flustered by the performances around the table. I guess he started to call me "Andy" and then tried to correct it to "Andrew," and what came out was "Andyrew." Catching himself — and possibly wanting to cover up — he made it sound as though he had purposely mispronounced my name, and repeated it with a little twist: "Andriu," he said, "you and I are going out to get a real steak." Before I could say anything, I found myself following him out of the dining room. He and I had a wonderful dinner that evening; we sat and talked till closing time in one of Dublin's finest pubs. The name "Andriu" stuck. Ed knew I didn't mind it; in fact, he might even have sensed that I liked it, and he never called me by any other name except when he introduced me to important people.

Now, here I was, in the first-class compartment of a plane bound for the Dominican Republic, hearing him call me "Andriu" again, and waiting for him to explain how and why he had lied to me. He took several more sips of the milk, perhaps to calm his ulcers, and turned to me again. "We are not going to the Dominican Republic."

I was baffled. "We are not?"

"No, Andriu." His face seemed somber. "I had to lie to you because we are going to Cuba."

"We're going where?" I asked, even before the full impact of his statement sank in.

First, I wondered why we were going to Cuba and why I had been told that we were going to the Dominican Republic. I knew there was a revolution in Cuba. In fact, for the past few days, the headlines said Havana was about to fall to the revolutionaries.

"I couldn't tell you where we were going," Ed continued, "because this is going to be a big scoop, a very big journalistic coup." He started to explain that he was to be the first American journalist to have an exclusive TV interview with Fidel Castro. The interview was going to air the following Sunday night on his show, and it was to be such a great event that Ed could not risk news of it leaking out. The cover story of President Trujillo was concocted, but in fact, the interview was going to be with Castro. He said now that we were in flight, he had to tell me the truth, and asked me to tell the rest of the crew.

I was perplexed and more than a little annoyed. Here I was, in the first-class compartment of an airliner, sipping tea, wearing a Saks Fifth Avenue suit, being flown into a revolution. Actually, the thought hit me that I was being kidnapped. I thought of my wife possibly having visions of me basking in the sun on some pristine Dominican beach, probably ogling some Caribbean beauties, when in fact I was flying into a revolution without her having the faintest idea where I really was, and without me having the slightest ability to let her know or do anything about it.

I turned to Ed. "My wife thinks I'm going to Ciudad Trujillo." Ed cut me off and held up his hand in a reassuring gesture. "Don't worry. At this very minute, my office is calling all the wives with a full explanation." He continued after a few seconds. "And there is no danger. The fighting in Cuba is over. Fidel has won the revolution and is in complete control." Somehow I didn't feel reassured, and I wondered if I could believe him. But he sounded honest and convincing as he continued: "My good friend, Jules Dubois, the Latin American correspondent of the Chicago Tribune, arranged this interview. He has been an admirer of Fidel — he is with Fidel now — and he is going to meet us at the Havana airport." Ed lapsed into his show-time style. "Tonight, we are going to have a reeeally nice meal and get a good night's sleep at the Havana Hilton, and tomorrow morning we will film the interview with the new head of Cuba."

The engines of the plane droned on, but their noise was locked out of my head by all the swirling thoughts of this sudden twist of events. I didn't like the idea of being misled. I was disappointed at not being trusted enough to keep something like this trip confidential. But above all, a new fear surfaced. I had researched information about electricity in the Dominican Republic, particularly at the presidential palace, as carefully and as completely as I could. I knew that 110 volts, 60 Hz electricity, exactly what I needed, was available at the palace, and that was my guide in the selection of the equipment I had put together for filming the interview. The thought crept into my mind: what if Cuba had a different standard in electricity and my equipment wouldn't work? Ed read my expression, of course without knowing what my real concern was. "Everything is going to be all right, Andriu!" He stood up. "Please tell the others," he said, and walked back to his seat.

When I filled Manny in, he was no less incredulous than I was. After I talked with the other crewmembers, I tried to doze and sort out my thoughts. The only thing I was sure about at that point was that without my knowledge and against my will, I was on my way to a revolution, the leader of which I was expected to photograph with equipment that possibly — very probably — was not going to work!

I was actually amazed that I could and did fall asleep, under the circumstances. As I woke some time later, I realized that the plane had landed and was sitting on the tarmac. We were in Havana. Though we probably hadn't been on the ground for very long, the Cuban heat and humidity built up rapidly inside the plane. The air-conditioning was off and there was no air coming out of the vents, as the engines were shut down and no auxiliary air-conditioning was hooked up to the plane. The plane's doors were closed, and none of the passengers was allowed to get off. Some of the passengers were trying to wave through the small windows of the plane, but obviously, they could not be seen by whoever was waiting for them at the railing on top of the terminal building. I don't know how long we sat in the almost unbearable heat in the plane — I don't even remember how long the flight took — but daylight was fading and some of the lights around the airport were coming on. The tarmac was crawling with armed revolutionaries. They all had beards and a variety of automatic weapons and wore what appeared to be an attempt at being in uniform. Without doing anything, they looked unfriendly and dangerous. I didn't like the scene.

Suddenly there was a commotion, and a group of revolutionaries came toward the plane. They were carrying a long, wooden ladder, following a civilian who, Ed remarked, was Jules Dubois. We heard the wooden ladder hit the side of the plane, and shortly afterward we heard banging on the door. A stewardess unlocked and opened the door. One of the revolutionaries jumped inside, leveling his submachine gun at the passengers. He yelled something in Spanish, and those passengers who were standing and obviously understood him sat down in a hurry. The next person coming up the ladder was Jules Dubois. He smiled as he spotted Ed, and the two shook hands. Within minutes I was off the plane, climbing down the rickety wooden ladder, carrying and balancing such personal items as my suit bag and my lightmeter case. No one besides our group was allowed to get off the plane.

Soon our luggage appeared, seemingly out of nowhere, as we stood by the plane with revolutionaries all around us, wondering what was next. Whatever it was, I had the satisfaction of knowing that at least I was dressed well enough in a Saks Fifth Avenue suit — drenched with perspiration, but still suitable to meet the new head of Cuba.

A young revolutionary came over to talk with Jules Dubois. He could have been an officer, as he seemed somewhat better groomed (though with the obligatory beard) and more intelligent than the rest of the soldiers around us. Jules introduced him to Ed. The young man explained in very good English that Fidel — everybody seemed to call Castro by his first name — sent his apologies, but he was being delayed en route to Havana because the people of all the towns and villages wanted him to speak to them. He was not expected to get to Havana for some days, and he suggested we meet him in Matanzas, one of the large cities some distance east of Havana. The young man further explained that Fidel had sent his personal airplane for us. One problem I saw was that Castro's personal pilot was so drunk he could hardly stand. I was relieved to notice that Ed didn't like the situation any better than I did. The whole matter was quickly resolved as we walked to Fidel's personal plane, which was a beat-up, small, twin-engine Cessna — too small to take us all, not to mention the large amount of gear we had with us. The young officer, if there was such a thing in the Cuban revolution, suggested we take cabs, though he apologized as he explained that the trip by car would take several hours. I personally didn't care, nor did Ed, nor, as far as I could tell, did any of the other members of the crew, as long as we didn't have to fly in Castro's personal plane, piloted by a shit-faced drunk.

Within minutes the revolutionaries rounded up six or seven taxicabs. We loaded up our gear and luggage and were ready to go. Ed rode ahead with Jules and the young officer. Manny and I squeezed into the back seat of the second cab, and Ernie and Jim, my gaffer, followed in the third cab. The rest of the cabs were stuffed with our equipment and personal luggage. In each of the cabs, a bearded revolutionary with a submachine gun sat next to the driver. Our guy, who spoke a little English, explained that he hadn't slept in three days because as his unit marched toward Havana, they had to mop up the last of the Batista forces.

Havana was fading into the darkness behind us. We were stopped several times by patrols, roadblocks — Fidelistas, as they were called, who surrounded our cab with weapons leveled at us. They looked every bit as rag-tag and tired as our escort did, which was a scary thought, and I prayed that their cocked weapons did not have hair triggers. Our escort dozed in the front seat as we bumped along some dirt roads, his submachine gun bouncing between his knees with the muzzle under his chin. He would wake as the cab changed gears, slowed down or stopped at roadblocks. After he cleared us through, we were waved on, except when we had to wait for a military unit going in the other direction. This was definitely not my idea of the Castro revolutionaries. I, like most Americans at that time, pictured the Castro army as a band of barefoot, bearded, ill-clothed and badly armed bandits in mountain hideouts. At least, that is the way they were portrayed in the newspapers and on TV. But as our cab was halted now and then, we saw tanks, heavy artillery and truck convoys, the real Castro army, going in the direction of Havana.

Several hours later, our escort told us we were coming into the city of Matanzas. We were getting into the typical outskirts of a Caribbean town, small houses and palm tree-lined streets, but the interesting thing I noticed was that there wasn't a single human being in sight. At first I thought it was because of the late hour, but in reality it was perhaps 9 or 10 o'clock. Then the cabdriver turned on the radio, and we could hear Castro making a speech to the people of Matanzas. Our escort explained that Fidel had probably started speaking around 6 o'clock or so; as was his custom, he was stopping at just about every town and giving marathon speeches on the way to his planned, triumphant entry into Havana.

Suddenly the taxi took a sharp turn as a bearded revolutionary directed us around the perimeter of the large town square.

We could now hear Castro over loudspeakers, speaking to a crowd that our escort estimated to be close to 100,000. The scene that greeted us was like one from the movie *Viva Zapata*, about a Mexican revolution. Machine-guns were set up on just about every rooftop, pointing down at the crowd in the square that was surrounded by revolutionaries, weapons at the ready. The square was jam-packed with people; all were looking up at a balcony on the second floor of one of the central buildings. Castro was speaking — shouting might be more correct — from the balcony, his arms flailing, stopping only for the thunderous applause that frequently interrupted his speech.

I felt helpless and had a twisting, gnawing feeling in the pit of my stomach. Here was an opportunity to record history, but the only camera I had was a large studio camera that needed 60-cycle, 110-volt AC, which at that moment I didn't have. What I would have given for a small, spring-driven camera, even an old-fashioned, World War II-vintage one! I would have liked to jump out of the cab, forge into the crowd and shoot endless footage of Castro waving his arms on that balcony and shots of the rapt faces, a few tears, whatever they were for. But I didn't have a hand-held camera. The camera I did have was a huge, Hollywood-type studio camera, which, without proper electricity, would not even have made a good anchor. Well, I consoled myself, I didn't come to Cuba to shoot newsreel, I came to film an interview, a big journalistic scoop, and even if I wasn't at the presidential palace in Ciudad Trujillo, I hoped to still do that — provided, of course, that I was going to be lucky enough to find 60-hz, 110-volt AC electricity wherever we did the filming.

The scene before me was truly amazing. For a moment, I forgot about the electricity. I was elated to be witnessing history, and in a strange way I was glad I had been kidnapped. Our cab, guided by the half-awake Fidelista — beard, cocked rifle, blood-shot eyes and all — pulled up to a side entrance of the building Castro was speaking from. Ed was somewhere inside with Jules, but the young officer was waiting for me and suggested that I come in and select a place to film the interview. I walked through the dimly lit, spacious and ornate corridors of the building, which was old, and my fears about the electricity returned. There were very few outlets in sight, and the ones I could see were old, round-pronged outlets one commonly finds in old buildings in Europe. Jim, my gaffer, didn't seem optimistic. I thought of tying into the building's main electric supply, but we didn't have tie-in equipment, nor did we have the cable that might be needed to bring the electricity to the filming site once we did tie in. The room the young officer suggested I check out must have been a meeting room for politicos in the past, but it was now empty, devoid of furniture, paintings and any other décor usually found in such rooms in this type of old, ornate public building. There were a few electric outlets, but they were built into the walls, eliminating the possibility of wiring directly into them. Then my worst fears were confirmed. My electrician told me that the outlets were wired for two-wire, 220-volt electricity, which could not be split and would not be compatible with our camera and sound equipment. I was devastated, and I knew that this assignment was a wrap!

But somebody up there, as they say, must like me, because nothing short of a miracle happened. As I wandered from room to room, I noticed that at one end of one of the wide corridors was a gleaming gem, a relatively new American water cooler, which, lo and behold, was plugged into an American-style wall outlet. I knew the plugs on my extension cables would fit; what I didn't know was whether the electricity was right or, if it was, whether there would be enough of it. Within minutes my electrician confirmed that, indeed, it was 110-volt AC, and it seemed to be wired with heavy-enough wires to power the camera and sound equipment. How many lights we could plug into it remained to be seen.

With the help of some Fidelistas — machine-guns dangling from their necks or shoulders — we started hauling our equipment up the old stairs and into the large, empty room near the balcony Castro was speaking from. Before long Manny had the camera assembled, loaded with film and ready to shoot. We put together and set up about six Colortran lights on their lightweight

PHOTO BY MANNY ALPERT.

Left to right: Ernie Zatorsky, me and Manny Alpert with Fidelistas.

stands, ready to go if the single outlet by the water cooler could supply the electricity. The distance from the water cooler to the room we were in was about a hundred feet. After plugging our two cords into the outlet (the water cooler having been disconnected), we posted a guard to make sure no one would unplug them. The fellow we selected seemed a good choice. He was big, full beard of course, automatic dangling from his neck, and had the strong body odor — a deterrent in itself — so characteristic of the

Fidelistas. If I saw him guarding the outlet, I would definitely not have tried to unplug the cords.

And thank God for all the extension cords I brought with me! I even had some left over after the camera, sound equipment and lights were all plugged in. I had the lights turned on one by one, and as the settings were stepped up on the transformers, the lights started to dim at the highest setting, which should have provided the brightest intensity. Fortunately, I didn't need all that intensity. The interview was to be filmed in black-and-white, and I sort of patted myself on the back for having had the foresight to bring several different types of negative stock, including some very sensitive types that I knew would allow me proper exposure even with low light levels. The lights were reset to the lowest transformer settings, which provided the least amount of light but were the most economical as far as the electricity was concerned.

Now came the supreme test: turning on the camera. With my heart pounding — visibly, through my sweat-drenched shirt — I stood behind the large studio camera, expecting all the lights to go out and perhaps send large sparks shooting out of the plugs connecting the extension cords as I flicked the camera switch to "on." But the lights didn't go out! They dimmed a bit as the camera, which normally would have been purring with proper speed a split second after it was switched on, began giving out labored groans, trying to get up to proper speed. I was delighted that the lights didn't go out, that the camera and the sound gear actually ran, but I also knew that if they did not run with the proper speed — 24 frames per second — instead of the interview we would have Fidel and Ed moving around like people in old silent films, both of them sounding like Bugs Bunny.

For those who may not know what a Mitchell BNC camera looked like or how it operated, let me simply say that it was a very large camera in an even larger housing, or blimp, that silenced the noise of the camera (hence the name Mitchell BNC: Blimped Noiseless Camera). The camera was operated by an electric motor that also powered the film magazine with a leather belt and pulleys. The pulley on the side of the film magazine was about

4 inches in diameter, and, perhaps for reasons of aesthetics, it had a series of small, round holes arranged in a circle. This pulley was reachable through a small, round door in the blimp housing. I opened this door and stuck my right index finger into one of the holes on the pulley, cranking it to add extra power in hopes of helping the electricity-starved motor. As I cranked the pulley, the camera slowly speeded up, and to my surprise and, I might add, great relief, Ernie Zatorsky confirmed a few seconds later that the sound-recording equipment and the camera had reached proper sound-recording speed, and, miracle of miracles, the speed seemed to be holding.

Now that I had a glimmer of hope of being able to photograph the interview, I had to focus my attention on how to stage the interview. When the project was first described to me — the President Trujillo version — I envisioned El Presidente Trujillo and Ed sitting in large armchairs in the typically opulent setting of a Central American dictatorship. But here I was, in a totally different venue, a big, empty room, existing on but a twinkle of hope, all built on the promise of a minimal amount of electricity — hardly what I would have visualized as the site of a big journalistic coup. I gathered my forces, as they say in some cheap novels, and Manny, Ernie, Jim and I led a squad of Fidelistas in search of furniture, any sort of decorations for a setting befitting a new head of state.

In view of the firepower behind me (literally), I didn't think this was going to be difficult, but we didn't have to resort to firepower. One of the rooms yielded a very large, old desk, and in other parts of the building we found some other items that I thought could be acceptable decorations for the interview. Somehow we muscled the old desk into the room. Castro was still haranguing the crowd below his balcony as we positioned the desk in one of the corners. I thought Castro might sit on the edge of the desk in a casual pose as Ed stood in front of the desk, interviewing him. Having decided on these positions, I used one of my lamps as a backlight, which gave the picture a bit of polish. I worked out the signals with Ernie Zatorsky, who would monitor the speed of the camera and signal me when it got up to sound speed or, in the unthinkable event, lost sync-sound speed. Jim, my electrician, knew to turn the lights off when we were not filming to keep the circuit from overheating and possibly blowing the fuse under the excessive load, and to turn them on again, one by one, just before I rolled the camera again.

I then called Ed, showed him where I thought he and Castro should be, and told him that I would occasionally stop the camera to reload or put on a new lens for close-up coverage. I said that when I changed a lens, he should, as much as possible, repeat the question he had asked before the lens change to provide coverage and give the editors more than one shot to work with. Ed nodded his agreement. At that point, I didn't let on that we had a problem with the electricity, and that there was a better-than-average chance of the fuse blowing, putting us instantly out of business. Setting fire to the building was another possibility floating in the back of my mind, but at that stage I saw no point in revealing our situation. In my mind, I had long ago passed the point of no return, perhaps as far back as when I started preparing to film an interview in the Dominican Republic. I was hoping that the fuse would hold, that I would be able to film the interview, and I saw no reason why I should upset Ed or anyone else with a possibility that I hoped would not happen. The situation was touch and go; either it was going to work or it was not, but I made up my mind that it would have to.

Castro was still speaking. I muscled the huge camera to one of the windows and shot some footage of the crowd below us in the square, and some side views of Castro speaking on the balcony. The camera ran fine because the lights were not turned on for these shots. Castro droned on and on. I changed lenses, getting closer shots of Castro as he spoke and the crowd listening below, and when I could think of no other shots to shoot, I moved the camera back to its position in front of the desk and sat down on one of the camera cases, waiting for Castro.

It was getting to be midnight. My perspiration-soaked shirt had almost dried, so I put my necktie back on in anticipation of meeting the new head of Cuba. But Castro showed no signs of slowing down or finishing anytime soon. Ernie, Jim and even Ed, who was sitting on a camera case and talking with Jules, were getting more and more tired. It was way past my regular bedtime.

Finally, sometime after 1 in the morning, Castro finished speaking. We jumped to our feet, expecting him to come into the room, and I rehashed in my mind what to tell him about our setup and our cues. I figured the young officer was going to interpret, but that turned out not to be necessary. When Castro came in, he cheerfully said hello and told us in English that he was glad to see us, and thanked us for coming. I was amazed he spoke English. It turned out, I was told, that he had lived in the U.S. for some time during the mid-Fifties. I also found it amazing how fresh he looked and acted after being on the road to Havana for days, stopping and talking for hours at just about every little town along the way.

He was preceded and followed by a throng of his bodyguards, and suddenly the small room was filled with bearded, guntoting Fidelistas standing shoulder to shoulder behind and in front of the camera, around the lights, all over the room. The space behind the desk, the entire corner, was full of soldiers all looking into the camera, talking, waving their guns around and generally scaring the hell out of me. It seemed like there were hundreds of them. But we had to organize the interview. With the help of our young officer, the corner behind the desk was cleared, and it was explained to the soldiers that during the interview, everybody had to be quiet. I didn't want anybody smoking, but the room was already full of thick, acrid, cigar smoke.

Then, just as we were about to start, there was a loud explosion and a bright flash in the room. I never could have imagined so many guns pointing in so many directions in the hands of some very nervous, sleep-deprived and trigger-happy revolutionaries. The loud bang and flash was caused by one of my lights, which had been knocked over by one of the Fidelistas and exploded. I thought it was curtains for all of us, but the soldiers relaxed when the cause of the explosion was found. The light bulb was replaced in its fixture, my heart rate returned to somewhere just above normal, and once again we were ready to start filming. My finger was desperately turning the take-up pulley on the magazine, trying to coax the camera up to proper speed. It seemed to take forever for Ernie to nod his head, signaling me that we were running with sound speed and the camera was properly synchronized with the sound-recording equipment. I signaled Ed, who, looking straight into the camera, gave his introduction and then turned to Castro to start the interview.

Looking back on this experience, I find it amazing how little I remember about the actual interview. I guess the events of the day must have caught up with me, and that was the moment of truth. It was do or die — the interview was about to start, and I still didn't know if the camera was going to come up to speed and continue to run. I watched the lights with one eye to see if they were dimming, indicating that the circuit was heating up, and prayed silently that the fuse — if there was one somewhere in the building — wouldn't blow. At that point, those were the most important, overwhelming considerations for me. Fidel Castro, perhaps the most famous person in the world at that moment, stood with Ed Sullivan about 8 feet from me, but they might just as well have been on the other side of the moon. Though I saw them in the viewfinder of the camera, out of the corner of my eye I was watching Ernie, dreading the possibility that he would signal me that we lost sound speed and could not continue. But Ernie, I thanked God, seemed to be in a catatonic state. His eyes were transfixed on his instruments; now and then he adjusted a few knobs, but he didn't look at me, for which I was very, very grateful. The interview droned on. My heart was beating rapidly in my throat. Any louder, I thought, and the beats would be recorded on the sound track.

We got to the end of the first full load of film, and I had to stop the interview while Manny reloaded the camera. I also had him put on a tighter lens to hold a closer two-shot of Ed and Castro. God was looking out for me that night. My finger was hurting and started to bleed — the hole I had it in to crank the

Photo by Manny Alpert.

Ed Sullivan with Fidel Castro and Jules Dubois.

camera was a bit too small and had rough edges — but once again the camera came up to speed, and as Ernie signaled me, I signaled Ed to continue.

I shot load after load of film as Ed and Castro loosened up and the interview took on a more relaxed, spontaneous feeling. We even repeated some portions using different lenses, and I was amazed at how cooperative Castro was and how well he repeated some of the answers he had given earlier. I thought of the many professional actors I had worked with in the past who continually flubbed their lines, but Castro seemed to have no difficulty remembering unrehearsed answers to never-before-heard questions, repeating them almost verbatim, even when asked to repeat them over and over again.

Some of the soldiers were sleeping on their feet. Frankly, what kept me awake was anxiety over the camera running with sound speed and the unmentionable possibility of losing electricity altogether. The cocked guns around me took on secondary importance in light of the worst-case scenario of not being able to complete filming the interview. But the more film I shot, the more I was beginning to relax, hoping that at least we had some footage of Ed and Fidel Castro, the new head of Cuba. At that moment, the revolution I knew and cared little about was very low on the list of my priorities.

Then the second thing happened that was a bit hairy. Ed, with his usual deadpan expression, seemingly out of the blue asked (and I quote as closely as I can remember), "Fidel, back home in the States, people say you are a Communist. Are you a Communist?" Castro jumped off the edge of the desk and, being a tall man, towered over Ed. He almost violently ripped open his shirt and pulled out a large, gold crucifix on a heavy, gold chain. He waved the crucifix in Ed's face. "I am a Roman Catholic!" he bellowed. "How can I be a Communist?" I was scared out of my wits because some of the dozing Fidelistas awoke and, hearing their commander yelling, reached for their guns. But Ed's next question put a smile on Castro's face. The question, as best as I can remember it, went something like this: "Some also refer to you as the liberator, the George Washington, of your country. Are you the George Washington of Cuba?" Castro was visibly pleased with the question. He eased back on the edge of the desk, smiled, and took a long time to answer, but whatever he said I don't think was very significant, as I no longer remember it.

The interview went on, and the camera continued to run. Ernie gave no indication of trouble with the camera speed, and the fuse to the water-cooler outlet — if there was one — did not blow. Ed asked many more questions and Castro gave lengthy answers. Suddenly, a note was handed to Castro, who explained that he had to go. The interview was over. Ed signed off and, turning to the camera, shook hands with Castro. Before I realized it, Castro was gone. His Fidelistas evaporated and we were in an empty room once again, a little worse for the experience yet elated that it was over and the interview was, I hoped, "in the can."

I wrapped my bleeding finger with my handkerchief but couldn't shake my gnawing fears: Did I have the interview on film? Did the camera run consistently with the proper sound speed?

Was the footage well exposed and in sync with the sound track? I knew that sooner or later, I would have to tell Ed about the problems, that we might not have any usable footage, but felt that this was not the time. The time *should* have been as soon as he told me we weren't going to the Dominican Republic. At that time, I could have explained that I had prepared to film an interview in the presidential palace of Ciudad Trujillo, not in the middle of a revolution, in an old, abandoned courthouse somewhere in Cuba. As disconcerting as that news would have been, it would not have been as bad as letting Ed go ahead, knowing that the interview would work only with the greatest of luck or by a major miracle. I decided to keep mum and hope for the best.

The few Fidelistas who had accompanied us in the taxicabs were still with us, as was the young officer. With their help, we wrapped up our gear and loaded the cases into the waiting taxis. Several lengths of our extension cords had to be left behind — they had welded into the water-cooler outlet and were so hot we couldn't unplug them. So we just left them on the floor, hoping that they would cool down and not set the old building on fire.

The square was deserted, empty of the throng of people that had been there just a short while ago, and the machine-gun emplacements were gone from the rooftops. Only a few Fidelistas — sentries, obviously — lingered here and there, but they seemed totally disinterested in us.

Heading back to Havana, I was in the first cab with Ed and Jules Dubois. The young officer was in the front seat, fast asleep, dead to the world. Jules was explaining to Ed that the American public was vastly misinformed about Castro. He complained that his lengthy reports were edited down to a few paragraphs and appeared in the back pages of his paper. Likewise, he felt that other American papers and news services ignored Castro and the revolution, and the public image of Castro in the United States was that of an unimportant dissident revolutionary in command of a limited band of riff-raff. He thought the United States had missed the boat, perhaps because of its close ties with the Batista regime, and ventured that Castro, having been backed by the Communist nations of the world, would probably swing into the Communist camp. Looking back on this experience, it is not hard to see how right he was.

The first indications of daylight were gaining in the eastern sky behind us as our convoy of taxis made its way toward Havana. Now and then, a sentry or roadblock halted us, but the young officer cleared us through and promptly fell asleep again. I was nodding off, as were Ed and Jules, waking only when we were stopped or when the cab hit a bump, ground its gears or accelerated.

Havana was already visible in the distance when we spotted a man setting up a pushcart of the type street vendors use at curbside to sell hot dogs and the like. I no longer remember whose initiative it was to stop, but we pulled up alongside the cart, and Jules asked the man in Spanish if he had any food. The man said he only had one loaf of bread, some chorizo (a kind of a breakfast sausage) and some cheese. Ed told him to make us as many sandwiches as he could. A sorry second, I thought, to the feast Ed had promised on the plane, which we were supposed to have had at the Havana Hilton the night before. The man fired up his grill and cooked the sausage. It wasn't the most appetizing way of preparing food, but the sandwiches tasted great. I realized I hadn't eaten since lunch on the plane the day before. Even the warm, over-sweet soda tasted good as we pulled into the city in rapidly brightening daylight. The young officer awoke and explained that he had to make a quick stop at the sports stadium on our way to the Hilton.

Soon we were parked just outside one of the main gates of the huge stadium. As we waited for our escort to return, I saw a never-ending line of trucks loaded with people, civilians, entering the stadium. An equally uninterrupted line of empty trucks was coming out. From inside the stadium, an almost continuous staccato sound of automatic-weapons fire indicated that although the revolution was barely over, the retribution had already started. Having gone through World War II, witnessing similar situations, I knew the guns were not firing in celebration of victory. Our cab driver explained to Jules that this had been going on for the past couple of days, since the Fidelistas had taken over the city.

Everybody who was suspected of having been part of the Batista government, particularly of Batista's secret police, was brought in for questioning. He didn't go any further. Jules seemed to be very disturbed by what we were witnessing, but he was quiet. For me, the first chinks appeared in Fidel Castro's shining armor as the George Washington of Cuba.

The manager of the Havana Hilton greeted us. We didn't have to register. He escorted us to our rooms. Though I was ready to get to bed, I found myself listening as he talked with Ed about many of his friends who had been imprisoned by the Batista secret police, tortured and murdered. He himself, he told us, probably would have been arrested sooner or later, if it weren't for Fidel winning the revolution. His description of the Batista regime left very little for the imagination, and I wondered how the United States could have so completely miscalculated the situation. At the same time, once again calling on my personal experiences during World War II, I was wondering what the manager's real story might have been. Was he telling the truth or just switching tracks, trying to get on the right side of the new regime? But whatever his motivation might have been, the stories he told us about torture and persecution were bad. After a while, knowing that our plane was to leave just before noon and I had only a couple of hours to sleep, I excused myself.

As tired as I was, sleep did not come easily. I tossed and turned for a while, trying to sort out the events of the past 24 hours, unable to stop thinking about anything other than how, or if, my footage might turn out. Then I fell asleep. It seemed I was asleep for no more than a few minutes when there was a knock on my door; we were leaving for the airport in a half-hour. After a quick shower, I was ready to go, though I thought it probably would have been better if I had not gone to sleep at all. There was no time for breakfast, nor do I know if breakfast would have been available at the hotel. The city was in turmoil, but Jules or some-body else had organized taxicabs for our equipment and us. The young officer was still with us, and I was happy to see him as the one person influential enough to get me out of Cuba. I had a bad feeling about the place; I was tired and hungry and wanted to get out, go home. Other than bearded Fidelistas, there was hardly anybody on the streets to the airport.

But the scene at the airport was different. The grounds surrounding the terminal building were teeming with people. If it weren't for the young officer and some Fidelistas with weapons at the ready, I don't know how we would have gotten into the besieged terminal building. Inside, the scene was the same. A shoulder-to-shoulder, shoving, out-of-control mass of people was trying to get to the ticket counters, hoping to get on any plane no matter what the destination. Ed, Jules, the young officer and the rest of us were ushered into a corner of what might have been a VIP lounge only a week ago, but was now a mess. Unbelievably, it did have a little food kiosk, and Ed ordered scrambled eggs for me and milk for himself. He had ulcers, which I suspected must have been giving him a bad time by then. As I was gulping down the eggs, Ed noticed the makeshift bandage on my finger and wanted to know what it was.

Like it or not, the time had come to fill him in on the details of our shoot. I had to explain that I rubbed some of the skin off my finger while trying to get the camera up to speed during the interview. He wanted to know why I had to do that. A typical newsman, he was asking questions, one question leading to the next, wanting to get to the bottom of his curiosity. I had to tell him the whole story. Sooner or later I would have had to do it, and I thought this was as good a time as any. I started by describing the conversation with Clay, telling Ed that I had assembled the equipment for use in the presidential palace in Ciudad Trujillo. I told him that if I hadn't found the water cooler, we could not have photographed the interview. I told him about just barely being able to make it with minimal electricity to power our camera, sound and lights, and I even told him about the extension cords that we had to leave behind because they were fused into the outlet. It felt good getting this off my chest, and I hoped Ed would understand that the whole problem could have been avoided if he had trusted me enough to tell me the truth about where we were going and what our assignment was truly going to be. I would have guarded his secret, and we would have arrived in Cuba with the right equipment.

Ed listened without comment. I could just about see the wheels turning in his head as he mulled over the situation. After a while, he asked me very quietly, "Do we have the interview?" I wasn't prepared to give a positive, definitive answer. "I don't know," I said. I told him I knew we had quite a bit of film, which, according to Ernie's instruments, had run with proper sync-sound speed, and I knew that the exposure of the images had to be mostly right, or at least within correctable range. But I also knew, though I did not mention this to Ed, that an interview such as this would be totally useless without good-quality live sound. Narration accompanying silent footage would not work. I knew it, and I knew Ed knew it. We were both silent when I finished talking. Then a familiar-looking man came to our table and broke the silence by saying hello to Ed.

It was George Raft, the Hollywood actor, who was well known and famous for his portrayals of gangsters in movies. Some believed that he not only played gangsters in films, but was also a mobster in real life. I, of course, don't know this for a fact, but at that moment, after he sat down with us, he told Ed that he was a totally destroyed, penniless man. He owned and operated two casinos in Havana, but as Castro's revolutionaries took over the city, the Fidelistas closed down his casinos, confiscated his bank account and took his cash and most of his personal property. He was allowed to leave only because of his American passport, but with empty pockets and only what was on his back. I believe Ed gave him some money. The stories he told us about the revolution were exactly the opposite of the hotel manager's accounts. The Fidelistas took George Raft's employees away, and I couldn't help wondering if they might have been among the people on one of the trucks I saw entering the sports stadium.

It was well past noon, actually closer to 3 o'clock, and more than four hours past our scheduled departure time when we were called to board. The plane was full, but seats were held for us in the first-class compartment. The plane, just like the one we had arrived in, was extremely hot and humid, as the sun had been beating down on it for hours. The passengers, who must have been on board for some time, were sweating profusely. Now and then some Fidelistas came aboard, guns at the ready, checking passports. Some of the passengers were taken off the plane, many of them by considerable, brutal force. Through the windows we saw these passengers being formed into groups and taken away. It was getting near sunset when the plane's doors were finally closed, but we continued to sit on the tarmac for what seemed like a very long time. The engines finally started, cool air came out of the vents, and we taxied to the runway. Spontaneous applause broke out as the plane lifted off. I joined in and sensed the relief of many of the passengers, who were possibly escaping a rough time at the hands of the revolutionaries. I didn't know if they were innocent or guilty, but at that moment, that did not matter.

The next thing I knew, we were landing in Miami. Most of the passengers got off. When we took off again, the plane was almost empty. I wanted to sleep and tried, but couldn't. Ed's eyes were closed, but I didn't think he was asleep, either. The events of the past two days were swirling around in my head. The anticipation of going to the Dominican Republic but winding up in Cuba; thinking that my wife might be upset knowing that I had gone to Cuba without telling her; having equipment for filming in the presidential palace of Ciudad Trujillo that was all wrong to film in Cuba in the middle of a revolution; the anxiety over finding the right type of electricity for the equipment I did have; meeting Castro; the scare of the exploding light bulb; seeing truckloads of people being swallowed up by the immense sports stadium and hearing the gunshots that most probably were mass executions; and having had very little food and sleep for going on 48 hours had me all wound up, and kept me from falling asleep. Twisting and turning in my seat and trying to force my eyes to stay shut didn't work. Sleep was impossible. The propellers droned on as I felt my ears pop, signaling that the plane was coming down. The lights of New York, a most beautiful sight, were coming closer, and shortly the squeal of the tires announced that we had landed. I was home. But my relief and elation were dampened by my uncertainty about whether I had the interview on film.

The CBS airport expediter had us in tow as soon as we got off the plane. We had already been cleared through customs — such was the power of CBS and a hit series like *The Ed Sullivan Show*. The traffic on the Van Wyck Expressway, one of the most congested thoroughfares in the New York area, had never looked so good. Ed and I were sitting in the back of the limo, he with a quart carton of milk in his hand, and I with six cans of exposed, possibly useless film on my lap. Manny did a good job of taping all the cans together. They were 1,000-foot loads, each running about 11 minutes. The total screen time of 6,000 feet of film is roughly an hour and 10 minutes. I knew the footage was going to be edited down to its essentials. What I didn't know was whether I had the essentials or not.

It was almost daylight when the limo pulled up in front of the Delmonico Hotel on Park Avenue, where Ed lived. As he got out of the limo, he turned back to me and, with his usual baleful expression, said, "Have that finger looked at by a doctor."

Ten or 15 minutes later, lugging the six cans of film, my suitcase and lightmeter case, I was at Movielab on the west side of Manhattan. The night manager of the lab, obviously having been advised by someone at CBS to expect the film, was waiting. When I turned over the six rolls of film, he seemed somewhat impatient, perhaps ready to go home after his night-long shift, and he told me that the film was going to be developed that evening. That was not good enough for me. I had been living with this nightmare, the lingering, gnawing doubts about the footage — Do we have anything? Is what we have usable? — and I wasn't prepared to wait till the following morning to find out. As it turned out, I had to.

Within the hierarchy of filmmaking, it was not my job to deliver film to the lab for developing. At the end of a work day, one of my assistants would pack up the exposed negative of the day, and either he or a production assistant would deliver the film to the lab. That was standard procedure. The film would be developed during the night and ready for the editors the following morning. The editors' routine functions with new footage are to sync the sound track to the picture, send it out to be edge-numbered, and then get the footage ready to be viewed as dailies sometime during the day. But standing there, listening to the night manager, all I could think of was the additional day's wait before I would know what I had — if, indeed, I had anything.

I told the manager I wanted the film developed right away. He didn't seem impressed by my needs and fought the issue for a while, but, perhaps because by that time in my career I was a better-than-average customer of the lab, he finally gave in. I told him I would wait in the small, ill-equipped receiving room and was to be notified as soon as the film came off the developing machine. Then I sat down on the beat-up, torn, Naugahyde-and-chrome bench, and within minutes fell asleep. Some time later, the manager was shaking my shoulder and I woke with a start. He told me the film was developed and the negative looked all right. The densitometry indicated that the exposure seemed in mid range, which was good news, but he told me that the beginning of each take, the footage just before the slate, was way overexposed, and he didn't have an explanation for the overexposure. But I did. My throbbing finger was a powerful reminder that, in fact, the film was just about hand-cranked through the camera, which is why the portion of the footage just before the slate, as the camera was running with lower-than-normal speed, was overexposed. In a way, this was good news, but it was only part of the story. The negative now had to be printed, turned over to the editors for syncing with the sound track and sent out to be edge-numbered, after which it could be determined whether the sound held sync with the picture. And for that information, I was going to have to wait till sometime in the late morning. I gave up.

I went down to the street and waved down the first cab that came my way. It took the driver, looking through his little book, some time to find out how much the fare would be to my house on Long Island and how to get there. It occurred to me how much easier it was to get a cab when a bearded revolutionary was doing the hailing with a submachine gun. Eventually we got to my house. I paid the cab driver and went inside to have my wife greet me: "How was the Dominican Republic?"

At first I thought she was kidding — having been told that I had gone to Cuba — but she wasn't. The Sullivan office never called her, nor did they, as I found out later, notify any of the wives. I was livid. I felt like calling Ed and letting him know what I thought, but I was home safe and sound, though tired, hungry and very sleepy. At that moment, it didn't occur to me that the experience of the past three days would probably become one of the most interesting and memorable in my career as a cinematographer. I took a quick shower and went to bed.

I don't think I was fully asleep when the editors called in the middle of the morning, but I was instantly wide awake and on pins and needles, waiting for the editor to tell me about the footage. All in all, it was good news. Most of the footage was in sync, though it kept going in and out here and there, but the editor thought that with all the coverage I shot, it was not going to be difficult to present the entire interview. I was relieved beyond description. Within seconds after I hung up, I was deeply asleep. When I woke sometime in the late afternoon, I told my wife the tale of the past three days. At first, I could tell, she had difficulty believing me, but as I related the details of the story, she seemed amazed — and not as annoyed as I was about the Ed Sullivan office not notifying her.

The big journalistic coup, the surprise interview on *The Ed Sullivan Show* the following night, was far less than I expected. To say the least, it was disappointing. For some reason or the other, the crowd shots and the shots of Castro speaking to the crowds below him did not end up in the version that was aired that Sunday evening. I still don't know why — it might have been the rigid time limitations of the show — but after Ed revealed that he had interviewed Fidel Castro just three days before in Cuba, the interview came on in a much-abbreviated form. The part about Castro being a Communist was left in, as was Ed comparing Castro to George Washington. Though I'm sure it was interesting to the show's audience, for me, perhaps because of the anxiety of the experience and the unusual circumstances of how the interview was accomplished, it came up short. It was a letdown.

I was disappointed and felt shortchanged at not seeing more of what had been so difficult, so traumatic to get. Of course, I had no right to expect the footage to reveal the personal drama of being kidnapped; the hectic improvisation, difficulties and anxieties of getting what we went for; and the tension of riding in a taxicab, wearing a perspiration-soaked Saks Fifth Avenue suit, in the middle of the night on some backwoods roads in Cuba with one of Castro's bearded revolutionaries. It all stayed with me over the years, and in retrospect, I am grateful for having been allowed to be a witness to and part of history in the making.

But during a lifetime of filmmaking, not all incidents had to do with problems connected to the project. Certain events in my life simply would not have happened if it hadn't been for circumstances on a film that offered up the opportunity for something unusual to happen. This was the case on another Ed Sullivan project in Alaska.

"… TO SIBERIA!"

We were filming in Juneau, Alaska, winding up our work in the Red Dog Saloon, ready to move the following day to Kotzebue above the Arctic Circle. Up to this point, working on this project, a high-budget, very popular television show, had been absolutely wonderful and enjoyable. In Kotzebue, we were going to film a husband-and-wife act a sensational performance by an acrobatic couple, atop a 100-foot-high steel pole. They were going to do all sorts of incredible acrobatic feats such as hand stands and spins while hanging by their teeth from the top of this pole, which, I was told, was made of very fine steel and would bend and sway dangerously during the performance. In fact, their performance was billed as a "sway-pole" act. To make this act even more interesting, the pole was to be erected at the edge of the frozen Kotzebue Sound, at a point from which Siberia could be seen on a clear day.

We were planning to operate four cameras, one of which was to focus exclusively on the amazed, astonished faces of about 1,000-plus Eskimos recruited from the area, who had obviously never seen such a performance and were therefore expected to be amazed. At the end of the performance, the pole was going to break — it had been rigged to do that — and, to the anticipated horror of the Eskimo audience, was to come crashing down. We were actually planning to do this hair-raising finale twice, with all four cameras focusing on the amazed-then-horrified expressions of the Eskimos the first time around; the second time, all four cameras were to focus on close coverage of the acrobats atop the swinging pole with only a few of the Eskimos in the frame.

Leading up to this performance, we were going to film a traditional Eskimo blanket-toss — a young woman being propelled high into the air by a circle of men holding a blanket — which, I was told, is part of the Eskimo culture and is performed at most festive occasions.

As we were finishing our last pieces of coverage in the Red Dog Saloon — a fiery rendition of the poem "The Shooting of Dan McGrew" by Robert W. Service, performed by a character actor who billed himself as Lord Buckley — one of our production managers, Paul somebody or other (I no longer remember his last name), came in with a sour expression on his face. This by itself was not altogether unusual, as Paul always had a sour expression, but as he was talking in hushed tones with our producer/director, Bob Precht, I sensed that whatever he was telling Bob was not good news.

We had been filming this show in Alaska for a couple of weeks by that time; it was an Ed Sullivan special that eventually aired on December 7, 1958. The show was part of Ed's program of bringing entertainment to people in military service. The main portion of the show had already been filmed at the theater at Elmendorf Air Force Base near Anchorage, where Ed introduced the acts in his typical fashion, the same as on his regular Sunday night show. The variety acts were performed and filmed before a live audience of servicemen. Other sequences rounding out the show were filmed around the base and various other parts of Alaska. For instance, the song "I'm Sitting on Top of the World" was to be performed at the Mendenhall Glacier by a very beautiful young singer, Jill Corey. The other numbers, such as the one we were going to film in Kotzebue and the one we were finishing in the Red Dog Saloon in Juneau, were going to be introduced by Ed from the New York stage when the special aired.

According to our scenario, the show was to start with spectacular aerial footage under the usual opening titles. At the end of the title sequence, Ed was to arrive at the base in a two-seat fighter plane. The plane would be seen landing and taxiing to a stop in front of the cameras, the canopy would open, and Ed would be

seen getting out of the plane and being greeted in a short ceremony by the commanding general of the base. I don't think I have
to tell you that Ed had not been brought to Elmendorf in a fighter
plane. He got into the plane just out of camera range, and then the
plane taxied to its camera position and Ed got out. But the shots
preceding his "arrival"— footage photographed from a plane
flying at near-supersonic speeds around Mount McKinley, over
the magnificent Alaskan mountain ranges, low over the endless
tundra and snowfields, and at other spectacular Alaskan sights —
were photographed by me. An appropriate commentary by Ed was
to accompany these shots as the plane looped and rolled until the
end of the titles, and as it taxied to its position in front of the
cameras and Ed got out.

It was tremendous fun photographing these aerial shots.
I'd done a lot of aerial photography before, but this time I was in
a supersonic fighter trainer, and the landscape below me — or, at
times, above me as we looped — was spectacular. Even being a
pilot myself did not prepare me for the experience of the high
altitude and flying at near-supersonic speeds, ahead of the roar of
the plane's powerful engines. Sitting in a completely quiet, vibra-
tion-free airplane as though suspended motionless under a deep
blue-black sky with brilliant, sparkling white snowfields below
was an incredible experience — one to be added to the list of
wonderful experiences the movie business allowed me to have. I
was sitting alongside the pilot in an F-103 Delta wing trainer,
holding a small hand-held Arriflex camera that weighed a ton as
the plane pulled several Gs in some of the maneuvers. I don't
know how I managed to hold onto it. In reality, the camera
weighs roughly 16 pounds, but at three Gs, that is roughly 48
pounds. Holding 48 pounds steady while looking through the
finder is no small matter under any circumstances, but it's even
more difficult when one is tightly strapped into a contoured seat
and wearing a bulky helmet with a visor, an oxygen mask, gloves
and a G-suit.

Flying at high altitudes over Alaska is an unforgettable
experience. The snow below is brilliant and endless, and the sky

above ranges from full black to deep, dark blue to a brilliant, luminescent band of aquamarine where it meets the horizon. We seemed to be suspended motionless as the plane rolled and the world spun around us.

But the most exciting part of the flight came after the landing. Our plane taxied into a high-security compound and came to a stop. As the canopy went up and the ground crew undid my harness, I noticed a military policeman standing next to the plane, just below me. He was waiting for me. He threw a snappy salute as I climbed down the ladder — I was wearing a borrowed helmet with captain's bars on it — and pointed at the side of the hangar where some of our crew were lined up, legs spread, hands high against the building as if they were trying to prevent it from falling over. They were surrounded by several MPs holding submachine guns at the ready. The MP explained that the men, having been arrested for being in a restricted, high-security area, had told him that I could identify them and explain why they were in a restricted area without orders or any other sort of proper ID. I could and did identify them; they were part of the Ed Sullivan crew. Though they had no real function during this phase of the photography — one of them, Bill Hermann, was a make-up man, for instance — they came along just for the fun of it. But the compound, which held the then-new and top-secret F-103 aircraft, was restricted, and even some high-ranking Air Force officers who were working with us on the show had no clearance to enter it. I noticed then that the high fences surrounding the compound were topped with concertina wire and had many large signs declaring it a "Restricted Area." Our vehicle had been cleared through the gates when we arrived in the morning, but after I suited up and we took off, someone noticed a bunch of strangely clothed people, our crew, wearing military parkas (loaners from the Air Force), blue jeans and a variety of the wrong kinds of boots and hats. It didn't take long for the MPs to show up. When the MP realized that the captain's bars really didn't belong to me, and that I had just stepped out of a top-secret fighter trainer with a camera in my hand, he became, understandably, nervous. He seemed perplexed — I'm sure this was not a situation described in his training manual. Even my pilot, who, of course, was a genuine Air Force officer and obviously had top-secret clearance, was detained. But it wasn't long before we were cleared and taken back to our lodging.

Ed's participation in the filming at Elmendorf was "in the can," and now that the Juneau section of the filming was finishing, I was looking forward to moving on to our next location, Kotzebue. But I wondered whether Paul had brought bad news, and if so, what the bad news was. As was usual, the whole crew congregated at the hotel bar after the day's shooting wrapped and we had had a chance to clean up a bit. Bob Precht, Paul, several other people connected with the show and I had dinner together that evening, and Bob told us that the wife of the sway-pole acrobat had become ill and was flown to a hospital in Seattle. It was hoped, Bob said, that she would recover by the time we were ready to shoot their performance in Kotzebue and would join us there. It was also decided, as a worst-case scenario, that the act was going to be performed by her husband alone if she was unable to join us. The following morning, we flew to Kotzebue in an Air Force transport.

Kotzebue was less than I expected. It was a very small settlement of some Eskimos and a few European types who were living there for reasons of their own. Near the town, if you could call it that, was an Air Force installation. The mission of the Air Force at that time was to man a string of stations on the D.E.W. (Distant Early Warning) Line, which was a chain of radar sites monitoring possible Soviet missile attacks against the United States. I don't know how long a tour of duty at Kotzebue was for Air Force personnel, but after the excitement of being above the Arctic Circle and seeing spectacular Northern Lights had worn off, I was ready to leave. There wasn't much to do at Kotzebue. On most days the servicemen couldn't even venture outside the buildings because of the extreme cold, high winds and snow-blindness, which, we were told, could be so disorienting that one might lose one's sense of direction and get lost in an Arctic blizzard. We were warned against going outside alone even in clear weather because of dangerous sub-zero temperatures, and because of the minute-to-minute unpredictability of Arctic weather. The barracks, all the buildings on the base, were connected by enclosed, heated walkways that led to the mess or any other place one needed to go. But we had come to do a show, and even though the wife of the acrobat was still in the hospital in Seattle, we went ahead with the preparation. The 100-foot-high steel pole was already in place, but we couldn't photograph it. Though the weather was clear, sunny and bright during the very short days of the Arctic winter, the wind was so strong that the pole was bent over to one side, whipping around in the gusts. Siberia, some Air Force people told me, could be seen on clear days across the frozen Kotzebue Sound, but even with the greatest of desire and imagination, I couldn't see more than what appeared to be a thin, horizontal line, slightly darker than the ice or the sky above the frozen sea. Not very exciting.

The first problem surfaced when we discovered that our cameras would not run in the cold weather. I guess the technicians in Hollywood had winterized them according to their interpretation of winter, which, even some distance north of Los Angeles, couldn't compare with winter above the Arctic Circle. The only solution that offered some hope was to put the cameras into covered military trucks and pump hot air into the trucks. Though this technique worked, it limited the cameras to stationary positions, which at that point was academic because the winds were still bending the steel pole way out of shape, and any attempt to film the acrobatic performance was out of the question. In a way, this gave us a bit of extra time and hope that by the time the winds died down, the acrobat's wife would have be from the hospital. We simply revamped our plans and decided to film the blanket-toss in the village as an independent act.

The trucks with the cameras inside pulled up at the village square, which was really not a "village square" in the normal sense. It was a snowfield that had a few huts, smoke coming out of their chimneys, in the background. The "crowd of Eskimos" turned out to be considerably fewer than a thousand. I counted just over 20, including the young woman who was going to be tossed. We shot some close-ups of a few Eskimos with weather-beaten faces beating on hoops that had walrus rawhide stretched over them. They chanted as they beat out a rhythm, similar to the sound of Indian drums in early Westerns, "Duh-da dah-dum … duh-da dah-dum," and they chanted something that sounded like: "Yeahhhhh-ahhh-ahhhh, Yeahhhhh-ahhh-ahhhh," with emphasis on the "Yeahhhhh," in cadence with the hoops. It was interesting if you had never seen or heard it before, and that may be the reason why so many of the expected Eskimos, who must have heard and seen this ceremony before, did not materialize. We filmed the blanket-toss as well as we could from the trucks, but as we repeated some of the shots from different angles, the Eskimos, who perhaps believed that one blanket-toss per day was enough (it is!), simply turned and left.

The one thing that caught my eye was an Eskimo standing some distance from us next to a dogsled harnessed to a team of dogs. I asked our Eskimo interpreter to find out whether I could take a ride in the dogsled; it occurred to me that here I was, in the center of dogsled country, where dogsleds were still widely used for transportation, and I had never even been close to a dogsled, much less ridden in one. Some minutes later, the interpreter came back and told me that the owner of the sled would take me for a ride for $10. I figured this to be a good deal. In New York, just to go downtown from anywhere uptown in a taxi would cost that much or more, and I had done that hundreds of times. But at that moment, I didn't think I would have too many other opportunities to ride in a dogsled. I fished out a $10 bill, pulled up the fur-rimmed hood of my Air Force-supplied Arctic parka and headed for the dogsled. The interpreter introduced me (I think) to the owner of the sled, who smiled (all Eskimos smile all the time), missing teeth and all. As the interpreter talked with the musher — dogsledders are called "mushers" — the musher had the blankest look on his face (under his smile), and I had the feeling that some things might be getting lost in the translation. I found out days later that there are hundreds of Eskimo dialects so different from one another that at times, even people in the same village can't talk to one another. More than a few of the Eskimos, I was told, have no concept of what the United States as a country means, have no idea of what national borders are; all they know is endless snowfields, and, I was told, they routinely come and go between Siberia and the United States. Although I didn't know it at that moment, I also was about to do just that.

The interpreter gestured for me to get into the sled. As I did, the musher tucked layer after layer of fur covers and beat-up, old, torn and ratty store-bought blankets around me. At first he wanted me to get under the blankets, which I didn't want to do for two reasons: one, it would have negated the whole effect of riding in the sled; and two, because of the smell of the blankets, even being partially covered by them was nearly unbearable. But the sled didn't move. I waited and looked at my interpreter for help, but he just stood there with the never-wavering smile on his face. Finally, I held up my right arm, waved it forward in the fashion of signaling a Cavalry charge (as in old Westerns) and yelled, "Go!" The interpreter smiled, bowed slightly, nodded his head and repeated, "Go, yes, go," his English not much better than his Eskimo might have been. But the musher got my meaning and yelled something like "Tcza!" and the sled took off with a lurch behind the yelping, barking, scrawny-looking dogs. The musher, one hand holding onto the sled, ran most of the time, and I wondered what would happen and how I would handle the situation if he tripped and fell and the dogs kept on going. It was not a pleasant thought, but he kept running on his short, bowed legs, occasionally yelling, "Tcza!" and before I knew it, the bouncing and bumping of the sled stopped and we were whipping along on what seemed like patches of light-snow-covered, mirror-smooth black ice between shallow snowdrifts, over what I thought might be the frozen water of Kotzebue Sound. I have no idea how fast a dogsled is capable of traveling, but we moved along at a pretty good clip, and the ice that was visible for a few seconds now and then just inches below me seemed to slide past with what seemed like incredible speed.

I wondered if I had overpaid my musher, or whether I should have bargained. After all, that was a way of life in some distant lands, and the first price quoted was seldom what was really expected. I consoled myself as I speculated how much this type of a ride (which of course would not be possible) would cost at Disneyland. Probably a lot more than $10. Though the wind was biting into my face, I refused to get any closer to the blankets than was absolutely necessary. The daylight was rapidly giving way to the early-afternoon Arctic darkness, and now that I'd had a new, fantastic experience to add to my list of unusual experiences, I signaled my musher to turn around and head back to Kotzebue.

At first I thought he hadn't seen me, and I let a few minutes go by before I waved my arm again. When this brought no results either, I waved more frantically and tried to turn and look back at him. It occurred to me that, indeed, he might have fallen, and the dogs, now without a driver and with me under a bunch of stinking blankets, were racing full-tilt toward Siberia. But he was there, standing on one of the runners of the sled, yelling "Tcza!" and grinning his ear-to-ear, toothless smile. Suddenly a thought crept into my mind: my $10 might have bought more than I'd bargained for. I mean, all I wanted to do was get a short ride in a real dogsled, but here I was, racing full speed ahead, and ahead was nothing but the frozen sea and, in the distance, shrouded in the deceptive darkness of dusk, Siberia. And Siberia was *definitely* not where I wanted to go. I kept emphatically pointing behind us, in the direction of Kotzebue, but the musher might not have seen it in the descending darkness, or his eyes, narrowed to slits, might have been shut by the blinding, wind-driven snow. And at that moment, a horrible thought hit me: this guy *did* think I wanted to go to Siberia.

One scenario after another flashed through my mind. I wondered how many Russian spies might do this routinely — come over to Kotzebue under smelly blankets on a dogsled, take pictures of the radar installations, and then hail the next dogsled back to Siberia. I wondered how many of our guys did the same in the opposite direction. Probably hundreds, I thought, but that was a very small consolation now that I was also heading in that direction. My thoughts wandered as I visualized myself being questioned by some KGB character, his pudgy, round face under a one-size-too-small hat pushed to the back of his head, and me in an oversized U.S. Air Force parka, looking like the Michelin Man and claiming to be a cameraman on *The Ed Sullivan Show*. "Vhat dis Ed Sullivan Show?" he would sneer, convinced that I was an American spy. Or possibly he would find out about my Hungarian background, and that I had skipped out of Hungary, a Soviet bloc country, while I was of military age. I could possibly spend the rest of my life in a gulag. No, this was not at all what I'd had in mind when I wanted to add $10 worth of dogsledding to my list of unusual experiences.

Almost automatically, my left hand started to grope for my wallet — not an easy task, considering that I was lying almost flat on my back in the narrow dogsled, wearing a parka roughly the size of the Goodyear blimp, and was tightly tucked under animal furs tanned with and reeking of rancid urine. But as difficult as it was, my hand soon extricated my wallet, and before the last vestiges of daylight disappeared I produced a $20 bill and waved it in the face of my Eskimo musher. He yelled something other than "Tcza!" and dug his heel into the shallow snowdrifts on top of the ice, sending up a cloud of fine ice crystals as the dogs stopped running and the sled magically came to a halt. We must have been, I fantasized, somewhere in the middle of the frozen waters between Alaska and Siberia (in reality, probably no more than a couple of miles). He reached for the twenty, but I pulled it back. "Kotzebue, Kotzebue," I said with as much emphasis as I could, pointing in the direction we came from. I toyed with the idea of somehow trying to explain to him that he'd get the twenty when I got to Kotzebue, but I doubted it would work. If he had misunderstood my Eskimo interpreter, who was speaking Eskimo, my chances of being understood didn't look good.

Under the circumstances, I gave up the idea as soon as I thought of it. I mean, I was now convinced that he had totally misunderstood my interpreter (who could have misunderstood me) when he arranged the ride. Trying to talk with my musher in English was, I knew, out of the question. My chances of communicating with him in sign language — though not much worse than my interpreter's language skills — were pretty slim due to the fading daylight and my confinement in the sled. I gave up trying to negotiate as soon as my musher mumbled something that could have as easily been "Vladivostok" as "Kotzebue," but he smiled and reached for the twenty, and I gave it to him. What else could I have done? Here I was, in the middle of nature's deep freeze somewhere above the Arctic Circle with night approaching, the temperature probably considerably lower than −20°, and the wind howling. I didn't think I was in a position to force the issue. I figured if he understood me and took me back to Kotzebue, all would be fine and well. If he took me to Siberia, I would just have to start learning Russian.

I also speculated that he might have misinterpreted my meaning and figured I was offering more money for him to go faster and get me to Siberia sooner. At that stage, whatever he had in mind I had no control over, and I had no other choice but to give him the money, wave my arms in the direction of Kotzebue and hope for the best. He yelled "Tcza!" again and the dogs took off. Then he yelled something I hadn't heard before, and I thought the dogs were making a wide 180-degree turn. It could have been my imagination (perhaps sparked by my optimistic nature, or my extreme desperation), but it did seem that, indeed, the wind, instead of hitting me in the face, lost some of its bite and was now coming from behind me. A glimmer of hope was rising, and I even thought that in the distance I saw some faint, flickering lights, and I hoped the dogs would not tire before we reached them. I wanted to get out of the sled, away from the blankets and the pungent, putrid smell of rancid urine. I wanted to get this new and unusual experience over with as quickly as possible.

There was no daylight left, though it was still early afternoon when the sled pulled up on the shore, which I hoped was the snow-covered North American continent and the Alaskan terra firma we'd left just a short while ago. Sure enough, in a few minutes we were back at the town square in Kotzebue. The blanket-tossers and the hoop-beating chanters were gone, as were the Air Force trucks with our cameras and crew. It was to my great relief that this was definitely not Siberia, but in a way it might just as well have been, because I had not the slightest idea how I was going to get to the Air Force base. In my haste to get a ride in the dogsled — and expecting the ride to last for no more than a few minutes — I hadn't told anybody that I was about to go halfway to Siberia. It was quite obvious nobody had missed me, and that everybody was now back at the base, probably on their third or fifth tax-free Martini. (Alaska was not a state yet, and at the officers' club on the base, drinks were incredibly inexpensive.) Fortunately for me, there was an Air Force vehicle at the village, and though it wasn't part of the trucks that were assigned to the show, the guys in it gave me a ride back to the base.

The ride to the base and the rest of that day have long ago faded into oblivion; none of it must have been very interesting, and all of it probably paled in comparison to the main event of the day, which was my $30 dogsled ride, possibly to Siberia, over the frozen sea. Though I now know that traveling the 200-odd miles that separate Siberia from the Alaskan landmass at Kotzebue would not have been possible in a short time, I still speculate about the scenarios that might have occurred had I actually landed in Siberia. This book would probably not have happened, or if it had, it would have most likely been written in the Cyrillic alphabet.

I was back on good old U.S. soil, $30 down but immensely richer for the experience. At least, I know of no other person amongst my circle of friends and acquaintances who has ever had an experience even remotely similar. I was grateful to be in a business that I thoroughly enjoyed, that was so good to me, and that offered offbeat opportunities like an occasional ride in a dogsled.

And there was more good news when I got back to the base: the forecast for the next day was good enough to film the sway-pole act.

Morning came early the following day, and by the time we'd had breakfast and moved to the edge of the frozen Kotzebue Sound, where the pole was erected, the temperature had climbed to 20 degrees below zero. The problem was that the wind was still howling, bending the pole way over. The huge, yellow accordion hoses were dumping hot air into the trucks; we were comfortable and the cameras ran faultlessly, but I wondered how our acrobat was going to manage the wind and perform his act in the numbing cold. The Eskimos were arriving, herded by Paul and some of our other production people, assisted by our smiling interpreters. All in all, about 20 Eskimos showed up. They were the same moth-eaten variety we'd had at the blanket-toss the day before, clad in patched-up, worn, seal parkas with hoods or in greasy, store-bought garments. Their heavy mukluks were not any better, but all of them were smiling, showing an astonishing lack of teeth. This crowd was also far short of the expected 1,000-plus, but it was all we had, and again, we had to be thankful.

Even before the performance started, we shot all sorts of footage, trying to make 20-odd Eskimos appear to be more — with, I might add, very little success. But by far, the biggest problem was that what we'd planned and hoped for, interesting reactions to the act, just did not happen. The Eskimos exhibited no interesting gestures or facial expressions; in fact, they showed no reaction at all during the performance. One after the other, the close-up cameras gave up on shooting the faces that all looked the same. The Eskimos were grinning constantly — at least, that's what we thought they were doing. We figured later that the constant wind and cold froze what looked like distorted smiles on their faces. Their eyes were barely visible; they were narrow slits under bushy eyebrows, unimpressed and disinterested blank stares reflecting not the slightest bit of emotion. I hoped, though I didn't really believe it, that at any point during the spectacular performance this would all change, but it didn't. The look and the reactions, or lack of reactions, remained the same from the moment our acrobat arrived and hopped out of the heated Air Force jeep. To my astonishment, he was wearing nothing but tight-fitting black leotards, a long-sleeved, skin-tight knit shirt and a cape. He bowed in the direction of the Eskimos, with their never-changing, blank stares. Maybe, I speculated, if the acrobat's wife were there in a skin-tight leotard, the Eskimos would have shown some interest.

I couldn't understand — and shudder to think of it even after all these years — how the acrobat didn't instantly turn into an icicle, but I was convinced he would within a very short time. But he smiled and, with a flourish, undid the black cape from around his neck and headed for the windswept, bent-over, 100-foot-high pole. I was absolutely certain that his hands would instantly freeze to the steel pole the moment he touched it. But this didn't happen, either. He was wearing what appeared to be thin kid gloves and seemed totally impervious to the elements as he started his ascent up the pole, occasionally pausing for dramatic effect and doing some acrobatic twists and turns. I expected him to lose his grip and fall any second, breaking into little pieces of ice crystals as he hit the rock-hard, frozen ground.

The editing of this footage was to intersperse his heart-stopping feats with the excited reactions of more than a thousand Eskimos. We managed to photograph but a few blank stares of a dozen-plus, bored-looking Eskimos, but, as the saying goes, "The show must go on," and it did. Somehow our magnificent acrobat got to the top of the pole — to the end of the pole would be a better way to describe it. Under his weight and driven by the fierce wind, the pole was bent almost 90 degrees out to the side, hanging over the ice-covered Bering Sea. I trained my camera's long lens right on his fingers, expecting them to give and send him crashing to his death. As probable as that seemed at the moment, the person in me hoped it wouldn't happen, while the photographer in me stood ready to record it, if such a horrible thing should happen. Thank God it didn't! Seeing the tiny, black-clad figure of a man atop a swaying, 100-foot-high pole in my viewfinder, being whipped by sub-zero winds that must have cut him to the bone, I was grateful that his wife was lying in a cozy bed in a warm hospital room in Seattle with pneumonia, or whatever illness it was that had saved her from the ordeal her husband was going through.

Finally, after many attempts to do handstands atop the wind-whipped, swaying pole, the act approached its finale and, right on cue, just as planned, the pole snapped in the middle. Like a giant swing, the top 50 feet of it came down in a broad arc, and I figured that, being twisted out to the side by the wind, it was going to crash into its base structure. To my great relief, I was wrong again. Somehow the pole, with the acrobat hanging on, slipped through the base structure — his head missing the snow-covered ground by mere inches — and went screaming almost all the way up to the top of its arc on the other side. It continued to swing up and down, over and over again until, its inertia having been spent, it finally came to a stop at the bottom. Our sway-pole acrobat jumped off and bowed toward the Eskimos. He seemed completely impervious to the numbing cold and, being the outstanding showman he so obviously was, he bowed and smiled as he assumed the classical stance of a world-class acrobat who has just finished his act: head held high, right arm extended upwards and out to the side slightly. The Eskimos, as was expected, smiled. (Or was it just a frozen grimace etched onto their faces by centuries of hardship and below-zero wind-chill factors north of the Arctic Circle?) They smiled their blank, expressionless grins and, possibly figuring that they had fulfilled their part of the bargain, turned and walked away. Our acrobat threw a final snappy salute at his departing audience and jumped into the waiting Air Force jeep.

But the full impact — the futility — of this incredible performance didn't come home to me until some time after the show had aired. None of the hardships were or could have been appreciated by the viewers; indeed, they weren't visible on the TV screen. How could one sitting in a comfortable armchair and watching TV in a cozy, warm room appreciate or even imagine the bone-numbing cold? And the swaying pole, whipped in every direction by the howling Arctic wind, looked like it was planned that way, part of the act. I don't remember exactly how long the performance took, but without the enthusiastic reactions of a thousand-plus Eskimos, the act was cut to only a few minutes.

The work in Alaska was over. Another Sullivan special was "in the can," and all that remained was going back to our quarters, returning the Air Force loaner garments, packing, having a few more tax-free drinks and dinner, and thinking about going home the following day. The memory of my dogsled adventure kept coming back to me. What if I had ended up in Siberia? I wouldn't be going home the next morning, and I wondered how the rest of my life would have turned out. But I will never forget the excitement or the toothless grin of my musher, and I will never cease to wonder how well he might have understood the situation. Well, it doesn't matter now, because all's well that ends well. Life mushes on. Tcza!

FRIENDS AND THEIR BOATS

Not all projects take one away from home to a revolution or to the frozen Arctic. Projects at times happen near one's home, family and friends. Many of my friends in my suburban neighborhood of Upper Brookville on Long Island, New York, know that I worked in the film and television industries, but I suspect very few really knew just what it was I did. Some of them, wealthy and successful businessmen, automatically assumed that I was as successful as they were; otherwise, how could I live in our affluent area? The truth is, the film industry was very good to me. I'm one of the few cinematographers who worked most of the time in a highly competitive freelance business, and I was fortunate to get some real plums, projects that were high profile, interesting and lucrative. The films I photographed were produced mostly by the big studios with top talent. If one had asked some of my neighbors what a cinematographer did, a few might have ventured a guess, but most would not have had the slightest idea. Strangely, quite a few believed I was some sort of a big shot, perhaps for no other reason than they didn't want to associate with anyone who was not. I made no special effort to dispel or reinforce that myth. Instead, whenever the situation came up, I would retreat behind a smile, which most of the time was misinterpreted as a silent concurrence.

Believing this myth, one very wealthy, elderly lady pursued me for years; she wanted me to make a movie about her family, which went back to the boat that followed the *Mayflower* to the shores of America. She thought, and told me again and again, that her family's history was interesting — which I learned later to be true — and couldn't understand that I had little (nothing, to put it more accurately) to do with selecting projects to be made into movies. I tried to tell her many times that marketing ideas, books or stories as potential subjects for films was an entirely different field from mine, but in the face of her relentless pursuit, and in a spirit to help her (perhaps to put an end to her pestering me), I suggested she write and publish her family's history, which could then be offered to the studios. As a result, she hired a writer and an archivist to research and write her family's story all the way back to the second boat that dropped anchor at Plymouth Rock. Her story was indeed very interesting, but it never went anywhere, not just because of my lack of ability to sell it, but also for many other reasons — one of which, I suspect, was that stories such as hers were not of interest to filmmakers or audiences at that time.

Many other people, also believing that all I needed to do was snap my fingers and whatever they wanted would instantly happen, approached me with requests. The most-often-asked favor would involve a son, daughter, cousin, son of a dear friend, "lovely young people," who all wanted to be in the film business — mostly starting as directors or cinematographers, or in some other top position. In the face of such requests, I'd generally agree to at least meet with the young person, usually on a Saturday or Sunday morning, have a cup of coffee, and, after a few minutes of conversation — after finding out that, in fact, he or she had not a clue about directing or photography — I'd generally advise the person to seek fame and fortune in another field.

There were some strange requests, also. Some of my neighbors wanted to have a movie company use their home as a location for a film. When the opportunity came up and I was able to play a role in having a local house selected as a location, particularly if it belonged to someone I knew, then when the movie company showed up with its endless caravan of trucks, equipment, lights, cameras, cast, crews and mobile dressing rooms, some found the glamour almost too much to deal with, and my importance as an influential member of the motion-picture and television community became indisputable. No cocktail party I attended would slip by without someone telling me about his or her house having recently been renovated, the kitchen redesigned or a new garage put on, hoping I would show up the following Monday followed by a procession of glamorous stars. And there were some goofy suggestions, too. More than a few neighbors had a pet, an adorable cat or canary, with extraordinary personal traits that the film industry just couldn't, or shouldn't, do without.

My noncommittal attitude helped me stonewall a man I met at a party who was a manufacturer of boats and wanted me to put his boats in a movie. A few of my friends claim that Frank Giovanelli was in the Mafia. Personally, I never thought of him as anything but a very regular, likeable guy, but his name in reality is not Frank Giovanelli. I'll call him that for the purposes of this story, just in case he is in the Mafia. I met Frank through a friend, a highly respected surgeon who lives not far from my house, whose daughter was a good friend and schoolmate of my daughter and Frank's daughter. Frank, I found out as time went by and we saw each other at parties, was in the boat-building business, amongst other ventures, and he never let an opportunity go by without reminding me, drink in hand, not to hesitate to call him if I ever needed a boat for a movie. Requests of this kind are not uncommon; actually, many manufacturers are anxious to put their products in films, and Hollywood is eager to get set dressings, props and some big-price-tag items like boats for their films. Both sides do well. The manufacturers get good PR, extremely valuable exposure for their products, and the studios get state-of-the-art and at times very valuable items to use in their films for free. In fact, this practice has gone so far in recent years that the studios have established "product placement/procurement departments," whose function is to not only get products needed by a production, but also get a financial contribution from the manufacturers for the film's budget. By getting their products into a movie and getting financially involved in the production, the manufacturers are also ensured favorable presentation of their product, as opposed to representation that could be detrimental. If and when a product has to be unfavorably presented because of the dictates of the story — for example, a computer that does not perform well — the studio usually goes to great lengths to present the item in a way that conceals its identity. This is not done exclusively out of kindness on the studio's part, but rather because an unfavorable portrayal might leave the studio exposed to lawsuits and bad publicity. Of course, computer-literate people would be able to identify a model even with its name plate removed and its looks altered, but even so, manufacturers would go to any end to avoid unfavorable exposure.

I was not surprised when Frank offered one of his boats, but I *was* surprised when the need for a boat in a movie unexpectedly came up. Not too long after the party where I last talked with Frank, I was offered the movie *Remo Williams: The Adventure Begins.* It was an independently produced, high-budget adventure film that hoped to become America's answer to the James Bond movies, with Fred Ward in the lead, playing a super-secret government agent. The film also starred Wilford Brimley, Joel Grey, Kate Mulgrew and a few other notables, and depicted the somewhat lame story of a super-secret agency whose mission it was to rid the world of some bad people without, in Brimley's words, "embarrassing the president." The film was based on a very successful series of paperback books, *The Destroyer.* Much of the film's exciting action took place around and on the Statue of Liberty, which, during the filming of the movie, was undergoing renovation. It was surrounded with scaffolding, the vital ingredient of hair-raising stunts and chases designed by the film's director, Guy Hamilton, who was well known for his work on James Bond movies. We even built a replica of the Statue of Liberty from the chest up in Mexico so the scaffolding could be positioned to facilitate the execution of the stunts.

But most of the photography around and involving the real statue was to be filmed in New York Harbor, which is where a boat was needed. The boat was only going to be used as the getaway vehicle by the film's heavies (the bad guys in movies are called "heavies"), who, after giving Fred Ward a hard time, leave the Statue of Liberty in the boat. The script called for a speedboat, a Cigarette-class ocean racer much favored for its speed by wealthy sportsmen and drug smugglers. Because manufacturers often shy away from having their products used in connection with questionable characters such as drug runners — or, in the case of *Remo Williams: The Adventure Begins*, the heavies — I wasn't terribly anxious to press Frank for a boat. I didn't think he would want his product associated with the film's bad guys. I also speculated that he probably had a less expensive boat in mind when he made his numerous offers on alcohol-hazed occasions. I didn't want to put him in a position where he would have to turn me down, yet when the issue of the boat came up, I suggested to our property chief (the fellow responsible for lining up and getting the property needs of a film) that he contact Frank Giovanelli and encouraged him to use my name. Our property master was also of Italian descent — his (real) name is Tom Saccio. It's not that I thought his Italian ancestry would have any bearing on the situation, but I hoped that the two of them would get along. They did!

Tom Saccio told me that Frank Giovanelli could not have been nicer. He invited Tom to lunch and told him he would give us any kind of boat we wanted. Needless to say, the producers of the picture, Judy Goldstein and Larry Spiegel, were also delighted. They could have rented a boat, and in fact, as is the case with most picture props, they were planning to do just that; but finding and renting a boat of that type in the New York area would not have been easy. Those types of boats are very expensive, and transporting one to and from the location would have called for lots of difficult and expensive logistical arrangements. Frank Giovanelli not only promised the right kind of boat for free, he also offered to bring it to our location and take it away when we were finished with it. He didn't even ask for an insurance waver. Everybody was happy, and I was the hero of the day for helping to bring about such a wonderful deal.

Our work at the statue continued. Day after day, we showed up at the New York Fire Department dock at the crack of dawn and were ferried to the statue in a small tugboat. The statue and the island it stands on were closed to the public at that time due to the restoration work. Working on the scaffolding next to the gigantic statue was interesting for the first couple of days, but the miseries of the job soon overshadowed the excitement. It was cold, and the constant wind whipping through New York Harbor froze our faces and cut us to the bone. Wearing bulky, foul-weather gear plus safety harnesses (we had to latch onto the scaffolding wherever we worked) made the work tedious and difficult. And as we got deeper and deeper into winter, the weather deteriorated. But as the saying goes, "the show must go on," and it did. We accomplished a bit every day —not always our full assigned quota, but we kept inching ahead.

Frank Giovanelli's boat arrived at the Statue of Liberty on the designated day. It was a beautiful and obviously very expensive Cigarette-class boat, and it was tied up alongside the ferry slip. The U.S. Parks Department maintains slips for its own boats and allowed us to use one while the Cigarette was at the statue. There was much ooh-ing and aah-ing as we all went aboard and admired the boat's beautiful appointments — its brightwork, cabin, instruments, controls and so on. The problem was that we were so hopelessly behind in our schedule that we knew we wouldn't be able to get to the boat scenes that day, or for some time to come. Besides, the forecast was bad for the following day, and the boat scenes called for good weather. As it turned out, the bad weather continued for a stretch of about four days. It rained hard, the wind blew with gale force and, unable to work, we fell further and further behind schedule.

We all started to feel bad about keeping the boat tied up in the slip — particularly when we found out that, in fact, it did not belong to Frank Giovanelli. He had built the boat, but had sold it just a couple of weeks before he lent it to us. As it was the only boat of this type in the New York area, he had contacted its new owner and managed to borrow it for the duration of the filming. I'm not sure whether the owner of the boat had even seen the boat after he bought it, or if it had been delivered to him, or how this situation had been arranged. Frankly, looking back on this experience, I'm not even sure whether the boat's owner even knew he had loaned his expensive, new boat to a movie company, or that his expensive, new boat was tied to four piles at the Statue of Liberty, bouncing and heaving in a small slip, whipped by the gale-force winds, while the company was standing down. But the weather finally cleared enough for us to resume work, and the schedule was readjusted so the boat scenes could be shot first in order to return the boat to Frank and get rid of the expensive liability it represented. The boat scenes were listed for the following morning.

There were still some clouds in the sky as our tug pulled away from the dock at the Fire Department, but, well rested by the stand-down, we were all looking forward to going back to work. The water in New York Harbor was still very choppy, and our little tug bobbed on the waves like a Ping-Pong ball as we crossed the harbor. It heaved left and right but finally rounded the statue, ready to tie up and let us off. I noticed that the Cigarette was no longer tied up in the slip and smiled inwardly at the super-efficient work ethics of Tommy Saccio, whom I had known and worked with for many years on many films, and who, I can vouch, is one of the best, if not *the* best, property masters in the business. I figured Tommy must have come to the statue early, ahead of us, in order to get the boat to its location at the filming site. I walked from the dock to the statue and the boat-scene location, but the boat wasn't there, either. Neither was Tommy. No one, including his crew, knew where he was or where the boat was. Slowly, a terrible, gnawing knot started to form in my stomach. I began to sense that in fact, everyone knew where Tommy and the boat were but didn't want to say. I tried hard not to let my suspicions get control of me, but it was to no avail. Nobody seemed to know where Tommy or the boat was. My suspicion that they *did* know was confirmed shortly. Here is how, over the rest of the morning, the full story got pieced together.

During the three days we weren't at the statue, the boat had taken on water in the gale winds and driving rain, even though it was covered. The bilge pump came on automatically, but the three days of continuous pumping must have depleted the battery, and the Cigarette slowly filled up with water and sank. When Tommy got to the statue ahead of the rest of the crew that morning, he couldn't see the boat; it was still there, tied to the four piles, but was now hanging from her ropes, completely out of sight, under about 8 feet of water. At first, Tommy told us some days after the excitement had worn off, he thought the boat had been stolen. It just wasn't where it was supposed to be: tied up in plain sight at the dock. When he found out where the boat actually was — after, I suppose, rejecting the idea of killing himself — he located some help in a nearby marina. Raising the boat at the statue was, for some reason, out of the question. It had to be towed underwater to the marina, somewhere on the Jersey Shore, where it was raised and the water was pumped out of it. Any hope of putting it back into service to film was obviously out of the question. Not only was there visible damage to the upholstery in the cabin and to the other appointments, but the engines, we were told, had to be taken out of the boat, and all other instrumentation and mechanical components had to be removed and totally reworked or replaced. The estimate of time needed to accomplish this work was several months, and the cost, for most of us, was unimaginable. To say the least, this was devastating news. The filming had to stand down and, worst of all, Frank Giovanelli had to be notified.

Tom Saccio suggested that I, as Frank's friend, should call him and give him the bad news. That was when the thought of Frank possibly being in the Mafia flashed into my mind. I had a mental image of myself floating under water, possibly next to the boat, perhaps wearing huge, cement overshoes or an anchor chain for a necktie. "You borrowed the boat," I told Tommy. "You were supposed to take care of it. It was your responsibility. *You* call him!" Tommy's expression clearly indicated that he had also considered the "cement overshoes" scenario. Somehow he worked up enough courage to call Frank Giovanelli that afternoon.

He came running back to us with an ear-to-ear smile. His

Me with camera operator Jeff Laszlo in front of Statue of Liberty replica built in Mexico for *Remo Williams: The Adventure Begins.*

story was nothing short of amazing. According to Tommy's out-of-breath account, Frank Giovanelli had listened to him as he, little by little, as carefully and diplomatically as he could, fed him the details of the Cigarette's sinking. He told Frank that while we hadn't been at the statue for three days, the wind and the rain must have filled the boat with water in spite of its cover, and the battery quitting had finally caused the boat to sink. When he finished his story, instead of a lightning bolt shooting out of the phone, the calm voice of Frank Giovanelli asked Tommy if this was going to hold up the production, and if we needed another boat. Tommy couldn't believe his ears, and neither could I. We were both tremendously relieved; in fact, the whole company was.

I had not the slightest idea how much a Cigarette-class boat cost. I figured it must be in the hundreds of thousands, and with the appointments our loaner boat had, perhaps even a million. Why did I have to be a hero, I asked myself. Why couldn't I keep my mouth shut and not meddle in an area that was none of my business? I was the director of photography of the movie, not a product procurer; why did I get mixed up in borrowing a million-dollar boat, which then sank? As relieved as I was to hear of Frank's unbelievably calm and good-natured reaction to the bad news, I still wasn't 100-percent convinced that my house wouldn't be burnt to the ground by the time I got home that evening. Tommy Saccio and the producers felt it would be all right to borrow a second boat, as long as Frank Giovanelli was so nice to offer it. Nobody discussed or speculated about how Frank was going to explain the sinking to and settle with the owner of the boat. His unbelievable reaction was reassuring, and I don't think any of us wanted to get further into the mess. I certainly didn't! We decided to accept Frank's offer of another boat and get the filming over with as soon as possible.

The second boat arrived the following morning. It wasn't half as big or as opulent as the first one, but was a very nice boat nevertheless. The sun came out as a nice finish to what could have been a nasty situation, and we finished shooting the boat scenes before mid-afternoon. I watched with great relief as the boat,

The camera crew in Liberty's crown.

rooster-tail and all, pulled away from the statue, headed back toward Frank Giovanelli's factory and finally disappeared in the distance around the southern-most point of Manhattan.

I wasn't looking forward to the next cocktail party Frank was sure to attend. I wasn't trying to avoid him; I knew that sooner or later I was going to see him again, and the issue of the boat sinking would come up. But Frank just smiled as, drink in hand, I brought up the subject, telling him how tremendously sorry I was about the boat sinking. He didn't seem to bat an eye; he sipped his drink, smiled and went on to another subject. Images of *The Godfather* flashed through my mind, and I thought it best not to pursue the subject any further.

After that incident, every time any of us from the crew of *Remo Williams: The Adventure Begins* got together, perhaps to work on another film, we always discussed the boat story. I know we always will. Though we were able to smile as the story was retold, in retrospect I still have difficulty totally understanding the easygoing attitude of Frank Giovanelli. Some time after the filming of *Remo Williams* was over and the film came and went, I made up my mind to get to the bottom of Frank's side of the story. But I haven't seen Frank for some time now. He seems to have disappeared, though his family is around. There are rumors that he might be out of circulation for some time. The rumors have it that ... well, who listens to rumors?

Boats sink, actors get hurt, and at times one has to look for unusual solutions to unusual problems. Tennis balls can be a big part of such a solution.

TENNIS BALLS

I'm an inventive sort. I have several patents issued to my name by the U.S. Patent Office and a closet full — literally — of models of things I've invented. I also have stacks of sketches of other inventions and ideas that have yet to get beyond the original-idea stage. They say that necessity is the mother of invention. This is very true, as most of the inventions in my closet, and some that progressed beyond the closet stage, were prompted by something I needed but couldn't get.

I have a very well-equipped woodworking and metal-working shop and have most of the skills to turn out high-quality items, one of which has been marketed worldwide. It was never a problem for me to make an accessory or an attachment for a camera that would enable me to do certain things, one I couldn't buy simply because no such thing existed. In those instances, I didn't have to carefully think out the item I needed, and I didn't have to have precise shop drawings with careful and exact measurements. I'd just go down to my shop in the basement of my home, reach into the scrap-barrel for a suitable piece of aluminum or other metal, put it in the chuck on the lathe or clamp it onto the milling machine, and work away until something like what existed in my mind would slowly take shape. If the piece turned out all right, or close to my idea of its purpose, I would then proceed to step two and make the next adjoining part. This process would continue unless something didn't work, at which time I'd scrap the piece, modify and remake it, or in some cases start from scratch.

The love of tools, the excitement of fixing and making things, gave me satisfaction and a sense of accomplishment from early childhood on and has stayed with me in later life. As the years passed, I honed my skills and enlarged my abilities to imagine and invent, and to recognize problems and come up with solutions for those problems. When I bought my first second-hand hammer at a very young age, I had no idea how important this interest would become in my later life.

The process of making movies, the graphic representation of life larger than it is, constantly calls for solutions to problems that come up on set almost every day. The creation of images that exist in the writer's imagination only and devising ways to accomplish the impossible (or sometimes just the mundane) constantly test the imagination of the cinematographer. Some problems are minor and have many possible solutions, but some are seemingly impossible, without obvious solutions. Because the execution of a movie, the committing of the images to film, falls within the responsibilities of the cinematographer, it is he who at those times suddenly finds himself the center of attention.

And so it was that a relatively simple, routine sequence — it read simply and routinely enough in the script — for the movie *First Blood*, the original of the Rambo series that stars Sylvester Stallone, suddenly presented a problem. Because the scene was straightforward and simple in its component elements, the problem was not obvious and wasn't detected in advance, as most production problems are. If you've seen the movie, you will recall, I'm sure, the scene of Rambo hanging by his fingernails from the jagged-rock wall of a gigantic, sheer cliff over a bottomless canyon while the sheriff's deputies are pursuing him. One of the deputies, armed with a high-powered rifle, is in a helicopter, taking potshots at Rambo, who is totally exposed and has nowhere to go.

The elements of a scene like this are usually basic and not difficult to accomplish. There are establishing shots that set up the situation and introduce important elements, such as the location in which the scene plays out. The scenic beauty and the element of danger have to be introduced, exaggerated and exploited, after which the shots that will tell the story are

Camera on ledge as chopper hovers in canyon.

photographed. As the scene plays, we see Rambo hanging from the cliff in distant shots that show his peril, and then, in close shots, we see the horror in his eyes as he looks down, followed by a shot of what he sees: the swirling river in the bottom of the canyon, way below him. Then we cut back to his close-up as he looks at the approaching helicopter. We cut to the helicopter in flight and see the deputy lean out of the bubble and level his rifle with a mean, sadistic smile on his face. My problems started at this point.

Because the helicopter was hovering in the middle of the huge canyon, there was no lens that could reach far enough for a well-composed close-up of the deputy. And even if there were, the copter was constantly moving, undulating up, down, sideways and in every direction, negating the possibility of making well-composed, sharp, close-up shots of the deputy and the pilot. To further complicate the situation, as the deputy argues with the pilot their anger and frustration reach a high level, which was a very important aspect of the drama and had to be photographed in what we call "close coverage." All such scenes are covered in this manner; it's routine, and most of the time it is easy — except when the two performers are in a small helicopter in midair as far as a half-mile from the camera. Yes, this is the moment when all eyes are on the cinematographer, asking with or without words: "Andy, how are we going to make those shots?"

In fact, there are many ways to make such shots. The helicopter is usually brought to a soundstage, where the scene is photographed and the dialogue recorded. The background — the mountains and the canyon — is composited into the shot later, in postproduction. But *First Blood* was photographed in the wilderness of British Columbia. We had no suitable studio, and expensive special effects were not budgeted; the shots had to be accomplished on location at the time the rest of the scene was photographed.

When the problem first surfaced, I remembered a relatively small but level piece of ground on a lip in the canyon at just about the height the helicopter was going to hover at during the portion of the scene we wanted to cover. This little piece of real estate, I thought, would be ideal for my purposes. I went back to it a number of times as we scouted for locations during the preproduction phase, and made it a point to take some of the people key to my scheme — some of our top construction people, the helicopter pilot and so on — with me. I thought we could land the chopper on this ledge and get close enough to it with our cameras to cover the scene of the deputy arguing with the pilot while he was shooting at Rambo. What I had to come up with was a way to realistically simulate the helicopter's motion in flight. That was the necessity that became the mother of my next invention.

Let me digress for a moment and say a few words about another element of filmmaking for which the film industry is well known, and for which it is often criticized and/or admired. It is, simply put, the excesses it indulges in. Many of these excesses are widely publicized, at times exaggerated and blown out of proportion, and at times they are rumored to be the fabrication of the overly fertile mind of a P.R. person. But wherever a movie company goes to film on location, it is expected to arrive with the most beautiful and glamorous stars surrounded by luxuries, living the good life and spreading the wealth in a way the locals envy and admire and at times think of as excessive, unnecessary and even foolish. And this is where the elements of my story begin to come together. Imagine the following scene in "real life."

A fellow walks into a relatively small sporting-goods store, the only sporting-goods store in town. The store is neat, orderly and clean, and the abundance of well-displayed merchandise reflects the pride of the owner. He smiles at his customer from behind the counter. "May I help you, sir?"

"Yeah, hi," the customer replies, looking around the store. "You sell tennis balls?"

"Sure do! The best." The pride and self-satisfaction are obvious in the owner's voice. "They come three to a pack. How many do you want?"

"A thousand," the customer says quietly, without even looking up.

After a moment of silence, the owner leans forward a bit over the counter and repeats, "How many?"

The reply comes again without hesitation. "A thousand, please, and they don't have to be the best quality. I want the cheapest balls you have."

The owner clears his throat again. "You did say a thousand, right?"

"Yes, I did. Cheap ones."

The owner clears his throat. "Well, I only carry the top three or four makes. But I don't have a thousand on hand."

"Could you order them for me?" the customer asks.

"Yes, sir!" The owner's confidence is returning. "I could have them in from Vancouver by the day after tomorrow." He then adds hesitatingly, "But an order as large as this …." He clears his throat again. "I need some sort of a deposit."

"Not a problem." The customer reaches for his wallet. "Actually, I'll pay you for the whole thing now, and when the balls come in you can send them over to my office."

The owner is much relieved, takes the customer's credit card and, in a matter of a few minutes, returns with the charge slip, which the customer signs. A smile returns to the owner's face. "You must be quite a tennis player," he says as he loosens up. "Do you run a tennis academy or something?"

The customer seems to be engrossed in examining a baseball mitt and answers without looking up. "Actually, I don't play tennis. The balls are not for playing tennis."

"They are not?" The owner is puzzled. "May I ask what you're going to do with them?"

"Yes, we are going to support a helicopter on them," the customer answers in the most natural, matter-of-fact tone.

This unexpected answer knocks the owner of the store back a bit. All he can do is repeat, "You are going to support a helicopter on them?!"

"That's right." The customer realizes that his answer calls for an explanation. "You see, I work for the movie company that's shooting a film in town." He looks at the incredulous face of the owner. "And we need to make a shot of this chopper in flight, but we can't get close enough to it to shoot the close-up coverage. So we are going to put the chopper on a gigantic 'Lazy Susan' made out of lumber and tennis balls to shoot the scene." He looks at the owner as though this explanation has completely cleared up the matter.

"I see," the owner says, but, of course, he doesn't. "I never knew how they did it." He still doesn't. He doesn't know how, why or where, but the conversation must go on — this is a big order, manna from heaven, and one in business has to take care of such good customers. "So you need a thousand tennis balls."

"Actually," the customer says, "we might need more, or may not even use all of them. We'll know when we test the rig."

The customer is about to leave but comes back from the door. "Say, I have an idea. We will only use the balls for a short time and they will not be damaged at all. They won't be beat up and won't look used at all. We can open the boxes very carefully, and when we finish with the balls we can put them back in the boxes, as good as new!"

Chopper on "Lazy Susan" created with tennis balls.

The owner doesn't know where this is leading. He is silent and puzzled as his customer continues, "Yes, the balls will be as good as new. And if you want them, I could sell them back to you at half your cost. You interested?"

This is too sudden. The owner of the store is rattled and doesn't know how to handle it. He finally stutters, "What if they don't look like new?"

The customer doesn't hesitate. "Whatever balls don't look new I'll give to you for a quarter a ball. You can sell them as used for half price. How about it?"

The owner is still rattled, but it seems to be a good deal if true, and he is tempted. "I don't know. I'd have to see the balls."

"Fair enough," says the customer as he extends a hand toward the owner, who cautiously takes it. The customer continues, "And I'll give you whatever balls you think are too bad and you can't sell. You can give them to the kids at the high school." As an afterthought, he adds, "And if you don't like the deal, you don't take any of the balls. Just walk away from it. Fair enough?"

The owner nods but is unable to talk. This is not an average, everyday-type business transaction for him.

"Send the balls over as soon as they come in," the customer says, and walks out of the store.

If this were a scene in a movie, the posters would say, "Based on a true incident" or "The scene you're about to see is real." And, of course, the scene *was* real. Although I wasn't there, did not witness it and can only guess about the conversation, I did instigate it, at least as far as the need for the tennis balls was concerned. Obviously, I have no knowledge of any kind of a deal to sell the tennis balls back to the dealer, though I have heard of similar arrangements; and if, by chance, such a deal was made, I had no interest in it other than I needed a thousand tennis balls and got them. Now let me explain how I intended to use them. Not being able to shoot close coverage of the helicopter in flight, far away in the middle of the canyon, was the problem that called for a solution, and the tennis balls were going to be part of the solution.

First, our construction department was going to build a sturdy platform and erect it at the edge of the clearing on a lip in the canyon. This platform, about 15'x15' square, was to be firmly anchored to the ground and have nine half-inflated, truck-tire inner tubes placed on top of it. Resting on these inner tubes was a 15'x15' tray secured to the base platform with bungee cords. The thousand tennis balls were to be placed on top of this tray. An identical tray was to be placed on the tennis balls — but upside-down — and the helicopter was to land in the center of this top tray. If you are as confused as the sporting-goods store's owner was, let me try to clear up how this contraption was to be used.

Once the chopper landed, our grips (film technicians who handle light construction, the motion of camera cranes and dollies, etc.), aided by the construction crew, were to rock the chopper with long levers attached to the bottom tray on top of the inner tubes, while other crew members were going to rotate the top tray, riding over the tennis balls in gentle, back-and-forth, arcing motions. The combined effect of these motions would simulate the motion of a chopper hovering in place in midair. In addition, as the scene was going on between the deputy and the pilot, the camera was going to move back and forth, rising and lowering slightly, to complete the sensation of the helicopter hovering in the middle of the canyon. Long shots of the chopper in actual flight were to be photographed separately and edited into the footage of the chopper on the "Lazy Susan."

The effect worked extremely well. In the finished film, the footage is so believable that I don't believe the average movie fan or even an experienced filmmaker would question it. The chopper, in fact, was actually moving. It rocked gently back and forth and side to side, as it would have in real flight, and it made slight but noticeable yawing motions as it rotated on the "Lazy Susan." The actors in the chopper reacted to these motions by balancing and leaning from side to side, just as they would have if the helicopter had been in real flight.

I could not have found the solution for filming the close coverage of this scene in any motion-picture textbook or manual. But as I understood the problem, the need for a solution culminated in the purchase of a thousand tennis balls that acted as the roller bearings of a 15'x15' "Lazy Susan."

Excesses such as purchasing a thousand tennis balls are not that unusual in the film industry. Everything — props, wardrobe and almost every item needed for filming — is purchased in multiples. One can hardly take a chance on having just one of an item that could be lost, misplaced or damaged, causing the whole production to stand down for the want of one item that had no backup. It is never unusual for a property man to buy an item in duplicates or even dozens at a time, but it would be very unusual for him to buy just one.

But making films is a strange business. The story of the thousand tennis balls is just one occurrence that happened during the filming of *First Blood*. Hardly a day would go by without something unusual or unexpected happening, and now that I have confused you with the tennis balls story, let me tell you briefly a few other unusual things that still stand out in my memory about filming Rambo.

One would think that a movie company has everything under control or, with its vast amounts of money, can purchase all that is needed for producing a motion picture. In this high-tech age, this is increasingly true, but when we filmed *First Blood* on a limited, "independent" budget, solutions to problems like the gigantic "Lazy Susan" rotating on a thousand tennis balls were achieved routinely on an almost daily basis. Sets built on sound-stages are generally designed to eliminate production problems; in fact, certain elements are designed and built into them to facilitate anticipated filming needs. But nothing could be further from the truth when a movie is filmed on location, particularly at a place as rugged as the mountains of British Columbia. Working in places like the Western Canadian Rockies, every step — literally — becomes a problem. Getting up and down steep mountainsides to position cameras and other equipment can and usually does become a difficult logistical undertaking, in some cases even an impossible one. But shots have to be made, and the word "impossible" is very seldom an option.

Rambo was still hanging some hundreds of feet above the raging river at the bottom of the canyon, still pursued by the sheriff's deputies and still being shot at by the deputy in the helicopter when it became obvious that in order to enhance his peril, we had to come up with a shot that showed him on the sheer rock wall, exposed to all the elements. This shot had to sell his dangerous, scary and hopeless situation, and it clearly had to instill fear in the audience. I knew the shot had to be filmed from above Rambo, looking straight down into the canyon from someplace in space, away from the rock wall, to show its formidable expanse.

But how does one hang a camera in space? Bringing a crane to this location was out of the question. We were in the center of a primeval northwestern rainforest, and there were no roads, or even trails, on the steep, rugged, rock-strewn mountainsides. Yet, as I said, the shot was essential to the success of the scene; it had to be made. The creative juices began to percolate again, and before long chainsaws were cutting long logs from nearby trees, and within minutes a jury-rigged boatswain's chair was dangling from a boom hanging in midair from an outrigger above the top edge of the canyon. Even looking at this contraption gripped one's heart with fear. But I instigated the making of this shot, and I knew that in good conscience I couldn't ask any of my camera operators to make it for me. I took off my bulky parka, and my grips tied all sorts of safety ropes around my waist and helped me get seated on the Rube Goldberg contraption with camera in hand. Within minutes, the yardarm, a log about 15 feet long, swung away from the lip of the canyon. There I was, suspended in midair, supported by the most makeshift of all contraptions, scared out of my wits, and about to shoot a key shot for a movie that, although it couldn't afford a safer or better piece of equipment at that moment, would earn mega-millions in the end.

Danger, accidents and the chance of injury are always foremost in one's mind in a profession where improvisation is par for the course, and where excitement and the portrayal of danger is a key element. All of us in the moviemaking business get caught up in the excitement of some situations and do things that none of us would even consider under normal conditions. All cinematographers want every shot to be more unusual, more interesting, more spectacular and memorable; that is our mission, and we will go to all ends to accomplish that. Somehow, looking through the viewfinder of a camera removes the elements of danger, separating the image from reality. Viewing the image framed on all four sides turns the world before the camera into make-believe, unreal, where "real" danger doesn't exist. Even stuntmen, who are usually very careful about designing stunts, go all out to make the stunts more frightening. I never could understand why seemingly normal people go into that profession, so prone to possibly fatal injuries. Indeed, when something didn't go according to calculations, Benny Dobbins, a key stunt coordinator and a good friend of many movies and years, was badly injured on one of the stunts in *First Blood*. In a way, I understand the mentality that motivates flirting with danger. We are aware of the dangers of certain situations, but the excitement of the challenge, the promise of successfully accomplishing an unusual shot, makes the adrenaline pump and urges us on. Even stars like Sylvester Stallone get caught up in that excitement. He is an athletic, well-coordinated person in the best of physical condition, but there is no need for him to do stunts. Indeed, no movie company wants to jeopardize the safety of its stars, or risk even slight injuries that would put the stars or other key people out of action. Yet when a star of Sly's caliber decides to do a stunt himself, the company can do little to stop him.

It sent shivers through my veins and raised goose bumps all over my skin to see Stallone hip deep in water in *First Blood*'s cave scene, with hundreds of rats all around him and as many as 10 or 15 on his shoulders and back. The rats were real, but not wild. They were tame, white, laboratory rats, their fur dyed to make them look like the wild variety, but to me, at least, they looked like rats, smelled like rats and were rats. But he was the star of the movie, the story called for rats, and, being the professional that he is, he did the scene, rats and all.

In another scene, Stallone wanted his face seen as he fell into the shot, having just jumped from the cliff face (done by a stuntman) and crashed through the branches of tall pine trees (done by a stuntman). As he fell to the ground, Stallone wanted to make sure the audience would recognize him *before* he hit the ground. When such a stunt is called for, the stuntman usually falls to the ground and the camera cuts to the actor as he rolls one more time and comes to face the camera with carefully applied dirt and bruises on his face. But Stallone wanted none of that. He was going to do the end of the stunt — crashing to the ground — himself.

The ground was carefully prepared; big and small rocks, pebbles, broken twigs and anything else an actor or stuntman could be injured by were removed, the ground was turned over and raked with an additional layer of sand and peat moss, and camouflage materials such as leaves were scattered over the area of impact. We were ready to film the shot. The cameras were in place; as was the practice before a dangerous stunt, they had been thoroughly tested to ensure they would run and the stunt would not have to be repeated. Stallone was helped up to a branch just

Me with Rambo (Sylvester Stallone).

above camera range. The cameras rolled, the director called "Action!" and Stallone came crashing down. His scream, which the script called for, turned into an agonized groan as he hit the ground with a sickening thud. His face was contorted with pain, and his hands and arms were pressed against his chest. I stood and watched what seemed like an Academy Award-caliber performance with admiration, but in fact, it wasn't acting. It didn't call for an expert to know that the man was hurt. Yet all of us around the camera, being professionals, knew enough not to jump in front of the rolling cameras to try to help him and ruin a shot that dumb luck had provided us, one that could never be duplicated. After a few long seconds, the seemingly lifeless body stirred, and Stallone went on with the rest of his action. Somehow he dragged himself to the trunk of the tree and sat with his back propped up by the tree trunk. That's what the script called for, and that's what he did. Minutes later, he was in an ambulance on his way to a nearby hospital with cracked ribs. Needless to say, it was a wrap for the day.

As we stood around trying to figure out what had happened, the "unforeseen" factor came into focus. No one took into consideration the fact that in the rainforest, everything was damp, covered with moss and moisture all the time. The high humidity permeated everything, including the branch Stallone was standing on while waiting for the director to call "Action." As he was about to push himself away from the tree, his feet slipped on the wet branch, he lost his balance, and his chest crashed onto the massive branch he was supposed to grab to break his fall before landing on the soft ground below him. Sly was out of action, and without our star, for the time being at least, the film was a wrap.

The "unanticipated" or "unforeseen" factor that lurks around every corner on every production shut us down for the day, and we altered our schedule to shoot around Stallone for some time while his cracked ribs healed. This "unforeseen" factor, which at times can be serious, even tragic, can also be quite humorous, particularly in retrospect. But when it does happen, it can still stop a production in its tracks, which is exactly what happened some years before *First Blood,* on a television project, *Shōgun,* in Japan.

SHŌGUN

As with most productions, *Shōgun* was also plagued by unfore-seen, unexpected disasters. It was a very involved project, a complex period piece with a largely Japanese and English cast and an immense Japanese and American crew. The shooting schedule was long, and the language barrier increased the inci-dence of misunderstandings and foul-ups. There were also some subtle — and dramatic — differences in work ethics on both sides that at times separated the two workforces that were unable, or unwilling, to accept each other's ways of doing their respective jobs. But in the end, language barrier and all, it came together to become a great experience. I considered myself very fortunate to be doing the work I loved, and as an additional perk, I was in Japan, learning about that part of the world, its culture and people. Meeting and becoming friends with James Clavell, whose books I loved for years before we met, was one of the high points. I couldn't believe my good fortune when I first heard I might have a chance to film *Shōgun*. Re-reading the book and reading the script for the movie filled me with antici-pation — and a certain anxiety about how filming some aspects of the story would be accomplished.

One of these aspects was the earthquake sequence, during which the ground was to heave and shake and gigantic fissures were to open up and swallow tents, horses and soldiers, including Toronaga (Toshiro Mifune), one of the story's main characters. Fortunately, we had Bob Dawson, Paramount Pictures' top special-effects expert, to design and prepare the earthquake sequence, as well as all of the other special effects. As he prepared

My "command post" at the earthquake shoot.

and built the earthquake effect at a remote location, it became more and more obvious that under his supervision, the sequence would become another routine aspect of the filming. His method of achieving those effects was straightforward, ingenious yet almost simple. For instance, the fissures that were to open up during the earthquake were trenches of various depths and widths. These trenches, carved by cascading rain run-off over the years, were covered by sheets of plywood arranged side by side running the full length of the trenches, some of which were a couple of hundred feet long. The inside edges of the plywood sheets met over the center of the trench. These edges were supported by 4'x4' vertical posts cut into two hinged sections called "weak-knees," which were going to be activated on cue by small, electrically fired explosive charges. There were hundreds of these weak-knees along the center of each trench. The plywood above them was covered with dirt, plants and rocks that were all native to the area. Bob and his assistants were going to fire the explosive charges in sequence during the filming so the fissures would open up at one end and rapidly travel along the entire length of the trenches. Tents, horses and soldiers were to fall and disappear into the trenches as the ground shook and dust filled the air. Every test of this system worked like a charm; it performed well and always the same way. It was realistic and reliable beyond expectation.

Then, for some reason I no longer remember (and perhaps never even knew), the shooting schedule was changed, and the photography of the earthquake scene was rescheduled for a later day. During that time, a monsoon hit our location, and the earthquake scene was pushed further down the shooting schedule. When the day finally arrived, the conditions could not have been better. I set up my command post on the top of one of the trucks, ready to activate a rather complex signaling system of colored flags to cue each camera positioned in strategic spots around the huge quake area. Radios were unreliable, and I didn't want to risk losing contact with my crew during the filming.

Finally, the moment arrived. The cameras were ready to go, and stuntmen (dressed as soldiers), horses, a field kitchen and tents stood on top of the plywood, all about to disappear into clouds of swirling dust coming up from the fissures. The cameras rolled on cue and Bob Dawson pushed the red button. Nothing happened. Here and there, small wisps of smoke came up through the dirt, but none of the fissures opened, none of tents collapsed, and none of the soldiers or horses fell into the trenches. No one was more astonished than Bob Dawson. This was his responsibility. As a longtime pro in the business, he knew what it meant to have hundreds of extras standing around, the whole company standing down with nothing to do, while he investigated the cause of the failure.

He crawled into one of the bigger trenches and within minutes reported on what had happened. During the rainstorm that postponed the shooting of the scene, gushing run-off from nearby hillsides carried tons and tons of mud into the trenches; the mud collected around the base of the weak-knees, and when it dried, it solidly set the bottom sections of the poles as though in cement. "No safe amount of explosive can budge the weak-knees,"

Bob reported. But the show had to go on, and his solution was to wrap a very long steel cable around the weak-knee supports in the trench and drag the cable with a bulldozer, collapsing the supports in order to create the effect of the fissures opening.

Me, after the rescue.

Then something else went wrong. As Bob crawled into the trench, dragging the cable, a section of the dirt-covered plywood collapsed right over him, pinning him to the ground. This was at one of the widest points of the trench, and as the support collapsed the sides of the trench sloughed off, burying Bob under a huge amount of gravel. Pandemonium broke out. I was able to get a bunch of people together and gather some ropes, timber, large "C" clamps and shovels, and soon we had a rescue operation going. After some furious shoveling, enough dirt was removed to raise the plywood and release the pressure on Bob, and we finally pulled him out from under a couple of tons of dirt. He was in bad shape but was on his way to a hospital in minutes. A few days later he returned to the trenches — no pun intended. The next time around, the effect worked, and the scene turned out to be one of the more interesting scenes of the show. The unforeseen, unexpected aspect of filmmaking proved once again that if something can go wrong in the course of making a movie, it probably will.

And I knew that this incident was not going to be the only thing to go wrong during the very long shooting schedule of *Shōgun*.

One Friday night, our schedule called for the photography of one of the most complicated scenes of the entire 12-hour minis-

Top: Shooting at sea during a storm. Bottom: The Black Ship.

Me with Toshiro Mifune.

Top: A geisha entertains Lady Mariko (Yoko Shimada) and Pilot Major Blackthorne (Richard Chamberlain). Bottom: Mariko's seppuku.

A beheading.

eries. Those of you who have seen the show might recall the scene where Toronaga and his entire entourage are trapped in Osaka Harbor. Toronaga successfully barters for some muskets from the captain of the Black Ship, and, using Pilot Major Blackthorne's (Richard Chamberlain) expertise and leadership, he has his samurai trained in the use of those firearms, which they use to break through the barricade of fishing boats that cut off Toronaga's escape to the sea. The scene was set up something like this:

We are in Osaka Bay. Besides Toronaga's seagoing galley, the scene includes a big, old Spanish galleon and a very large number of small fishing boats linked together with an immense bamboo rope, forming the barricade. As Toronaga's galley approaches this barricade, 30 or so of his samurai, equipped with the muskets, open up with a fusillade of gunfire from the bow of the galley, blasting an escape path through the barricade of boats. At the crucial moment, the command to fire is given by Blackthorne, who is standing in the center of the group of samurai. Chamberlain was to shout, "Fire, now!" on a cue from the director. The dramatic effect of gunfire, not seen till this moment in the show, is followed by the fishermen (played by Japanese stuntmen) falling, somersaulting and diving off the fishing boats, which capsize and are chopped to pieces by the intense and vicious gunfire. Having eliminated the obstacle of his escape, the once-again-victorious Toronaga sails out of the harbor, leaving chaos and havoc behind, and is swallowed up by the darkness of night. This is more or less how the scene was scripted and how it was supposed to play out.

But before I go into what actually did happen, let me talk a bit about what goes into the preparation of such an exciting scene. The scene read relatively simply in the script, which gave a brief description of the location, time of night, performers and necessary elements such as the ships, smaller boats and so on. We all look forward to filming such a scene, at times in anticipation of exciting action, and at times with dread of those factors that, for us filmmakers, have been known to spell disaster.

As a matter of routine, after a suitable location for the filming is found, the preparations start and a date is scheduled for the actual photography. Crew, cast, equipment, and large props — in this case, a 16th century Spanish galleon and a full-scale, seagoing Japanese galley — are brought to the site. To illustrate the enormity of such an undertaking, it took 70-plus days to sail our "Spanish" ship, a replica of Sir Francis Drake's ship *The Golden Hind*, from San Francisco to the location in Japan, and almost a year to build the period Japanese vessel. The logistics of this scene were immense, but as it turned out, that was the easy part.

All of the small fishing boats also had to be created; some were built from scratch, while many existing, similar boats were altered to look the way the period required. Once these boats were in place, they had to be rigged with what we in the film business call "bullet hits" or "squibs." Squibs are small, electrically fired explosive charges that splinter the wood and form holes where bullets have supposedly hit. Actors who were also to be hit by "gunfire" had to be similarly prepared. In most cases, these "hits," when placed on stuntmen, also contain bits of clothing and fake blood. The advance preparation for just this aspect of this scene — creating the bullet hits on the boats and the actors — called for a small army of special-effects people and took several weeks. Additional hours of preparation were needed in the days before and on the night of the shoot to apply these effects.

Now let me mention some of the difficulties, some specific, others general in nature. In the case of any motion-picture project, the script is scrutinized long before the actual shoot by an army of experts whose suggestions and observations bring about changes affecting the scenes — and, in fact, the entire picture. Such things as night work are frowned upon and are approved only in the most essential instances; night wages are at a premium, and overtime pay, the limited time suitable for photography and the difficulties of working in darkness can cause the cost of the production to skyrocket.

A few words about boats: plain and simple, working with boats in a movie is a pain. In fact, there is a saying heard often in movie circles: "Stay away from pictures with kids, cats, wild animals and boats." Even the best-trained animals can be unpredictable and even dangerous. Kids and boats never stay still, and because they move around constantly it is almost impossible to maintain pictorial composition or continuity. And the difficulties multiply as detail after detail is added.

We had two large boats and a string of smaller ones. Dealing with two cumbersome period boats without engines (the Japanese boat had 50 oarsmen) in one scene can be, and usually is, just about impossible. Add about 30 smaller boats, and you can imagine what can happen when these boats have to be positioned in specific spots within the frame and maneuvered on cue from here to there. In order, our difficulties were that we now had two hard-to-control large boats and 30 smaller ones, and we had to photograph them at night.

Communication is another very important element in the photography of such a scene. On a soundstage, after a scene is rehearsed, the director calls "Action!" and the actors and crew go through the rehearsed motions, and usually after a few "takes," the scene is "in the can." Most of the time, no communication is needed beyond "Action" and "Cut." At other times, when working with a large cast or involved action, or when shooting on location with action that is distant from the camera, radios are used to cue the actors and other elements like explosions, vehicles and so on. For this, one needs good radios and simple, standard procedures of communication.

For our scene in Japan, we had some very second-rate radios because at that time, even primitive CB radios were not permitted in that country. But our biggest communication problem was that all of our instructions had to be translated into Japanese before they were relayed by Japanese assistant directors to Japanese actors and technicians. Conversely, the Japanese cast and crew's messages had to be translated into English before they could be relayed to the English-speaking cast and crew. As we say in the business, "The plot thickens."

Our main cameras were positioned on a specially constructed, large camera barge, which, just like the other water-borne vessels, rolled, heaved and pitched on the swells and shifted position constantly. This being a night shoot, my powerful arc lights pumped their illumination from the distant shore, but as the boats constantly changed position, the lights had to be constantly readjusted. As we worked in the dark, trying to deal with a constantly changing situation and messages that at times lost their original meaning in the translation, the situation rapidly deteriorated into a nightmare. What else could possibly go wrong?

Plenty!

As you recall, earlier in this chapter I described what this scene was supposed to be about. Toronaga's galley was about to break through the blockade of the fishing boats as Blackthorne gave the command to his musket-bearing samurai: "Fire, now!" But before I go on, one more item has to be understood. Firearms used in motion-picture work are real guns altered to fire blanks. Naturally, this is true all over the world except in Japan. The Treaty of Unconditional Surrender signed at the end of World War II stipulated that no one in Japan may own firearms, though there were some exceptions, such as the police and the Self-Defense Forces of Japan. The period muskets we were going to use in our scene were specially constructed to circumvent this rule in a lawful manner: they were non-firing guns that looked real but produced a flash electronically. It took about 30 minutes to prepare each gun for multiple firings.

Darkness, water, constantly moving boats, badly translated and misunderstood communications, shifting cameras and lights, Mickey Mouse guns — indeed, the plot did thicken. By the time we arrived at the location, around 5 in the afternoon, most of the big elements — the Spanish galleon, the Japanese boat and the chain of fishing boats — were in place, put there by an army of workmen who had worked all day getting the scene ready. My camera crew and I started setting up the shots so that by the time we had dinner and darkness fell, everything was in place and ready to roll. The cameras, all loaded with the right type of film, tested and tested again, were on the barge, standing by for the big moment when Toronaga's boat smashed through the blockade. The special-effects people were standing by, ready to fire the boat-splintering squibs as soon as the muskets fired, and the stuntmen in the fishing boats, dressed as Japanese fishermen, were poised to fall, leap and somersault into the water, some to die heroic deaths. Blackthorne, poised dramatically behind his musket-bearing samurai, was ready to give the command: "Fire, now!" These were the only two English words that the Japanese film extras playing the samurai had been instructed to understand. They were told over and over again to listen for these two words, their cue to fire the muskets.

Just before midnight, the moment was finally right. The boats, actors, extras, stunt players, cameras, lights and so on were all in place, and Jerry London, our director, was about give the "Roll cameras!" command, when Richard Chamberlain called over, reminding Jerry to cue him at the right moment. Here is how this short, one-sided conversation went:

Richard: "Jerry, you'll let me know when to say 'Fire, now!' won't you?"

But before Jerry could reply, one of the eager and consci-entious samurai, who had been lying on his belly for a good hour by then, listening carefully for his cue, picked out Richard's words "Fire, now" and, as he had been instructed to do — and not understanding the rest of the conversation — fired his gun. Almost immediately, another samurai fired, then another and another, and in a matter of seconds, all the guns were blazing away. The Japanese special-effects crew also took their cue — the gunfire — and set off the charges that splintered the fishing boats and the hits spurting the fishermen's "blood." Most of the fishermen were in the water by this time, some trashing and "drowning," others floating face down, "dead."

One of the American assistant directors, realizing what was happening and what the implications were, was frantically screaming into his bullhorn: "No, no, don't fire, no, no!" But it was to no avail. In the din of gunfire and the crackle of exploding squibs, his words might have even aggravated the situation, because to the Japanese extras, "No, no, don't fire, no, no!" might have sounded like "Now, now, don't fire, now, now!" and they only understood the words "fire" and "now."

I yelled to the camera operators to switch on the cameras and grab (photograph) whatever they could, hoping to salvage at least some of the imagery unfolding before us, but it was useless. Everyone's attempts to try to bring this disaster under control were swallowed up by the ear-shattering, crackling gunfire; the noise, clamor and confusion of squibs going off; the anguished screams of "dying" samurai, and the cheers of the victorious ones.

It was almost comical to see the actors acting up a storm, just as they had rehearsed the scene, as Toronaga's boat headed for and smashed through the barricade of fishing boats. The water was churning with "dying," "drowning" samurai and "dead" bodies floating amongst the wreckage of this fiasco. The Spanish galleon at anchor rode the gentle swells, and the rescue boats were heading out into the bay to rescue the "bleeding," "drowning" and "dead" samurai, some of who were still carrying on Academy Award-caliber performances. Standing next to our speechless, flabbergasted director, Jerry London, I surveyed the carnage and knew that it would be weeks before this scene could be made ready again for filming. For that night, the filming was definitely a wrap.

Looking back on a career of some 50 years, the interesting thing is that not all big disasters happened on big productions. The size or importance of the show and its budget bear little relation to the enormity of its foul-ups. And that brings to mind an incident that happened on a much smaller production, with results that were just as disastrous.

60-FOOT WAVES

One wonderful benefit of being in cinematography is photographing an occasional television commercial in between larger projects.
Now, I know that some of us, including me, spend money on devices
that tune out the commercials as we watch our favorite television
shows, but shooting commercials is a different story. In the first place,
the pay is much better than it is on even some very big-budget films.
The accommodations and travel to some of the most interesting
corners of the world are first class, and even on those few occasions
when one finds oneself amongst difficult or hard-to-live-with people,
the job is never too long.

But there is one other reason why shooting TV commercials
is so desirable for cinematographers: the opportunity for experimentation. On most feature projects, even on megabucks pictures,
the cost of production is so high that jeopardizing the shooting
schedule by experimenting is not encouraged, even frowned upon.
Not so on television commercials. With hundreds, actually thousands of commercials bombarding the public and trying to sell
products, all advertisers want the most effective ads on the air. A
commercial may take months in development — shooting test
commercials, exposing them to focus groups — but the day the fully
developed version arrives at the soundstage or the location for final
shooting, all people involved in the development of the spot turn to
the director and the cinematographer (the two are often one and the
same) for fresh ideas and the interesting execution of images, hoping
that they can make the spots more interesting, more memorable
than other spots on the air. Memorable, clever, funny phrases or
vivid, outlandish images make people remember a commercial and

bring to mind the product it advertises. Most commercials rely on such images, and the cinematographer is encouraged to experiment in order to produce outlandish, unusual, interesting and spectacular images, some of which may not be desirable or even acceptable in feature films. However, some commercial techniques do find their way into feature films. In fact, since the early Fifties, the beginning of full-bore television advertising, the results of experimentation on commercials have greatly affected the look and photography of feature films. Old taboos were ignored, new practices were accepted and preferred, and working on television commercials became the great proving ground for cinematographers.

So just about a week or so after I had finished a feature and was almost at the stage when I usually get restless for the lack of anything to do, the phone rang. "Hi," said one of the world's friend-liest voices, with just a trace of foreign accent. "Is this Andy Laszlo I'm speaking with?" I assured him that it was, and he cut right to the point. "Would you like to go to Hawaii, Andy?" For a second, I thought he was a telemarketer, but something told me not to hang up. Instead, I said, "Yes," and waited for him to continue.

"This is Bengt," he said. "B-E-N-G-T." He explained that the "g" was silent, and that his name was pronounced like a piece of twisted iron, "Bent." It was, he told me, a Swedish name, which led me to believe that he was Swedish, but fortunately, he cleared that up before I could ask a dumb question. "I am a Swede," he said, "a producer/director of television commercials. My company was selected by one of New York's top advertising agencies to produce a very unique television commercial." The spot required a very high degree of camera expertise, which is why, he said, he was contacting me. "I have been a fan of your photography," Bengt told me, "and I've been hoping to work with you for some time." Needless to say, I was flattered, thanked him for the compliment and let him continue.

The commercial was for one of the nation's largest food companies, advertising a new breakfast supplement with the taste of chocolate milk that contained all the vitamins and minerals needed by a young body but didn't have the unhealthy qualities of some other breakfast foods. What was going to make this commercial so unique, so interesting, Bengt went on, was that the entire spot was to contain only two shots. Sixty seconds of screen time filled with just two shots — as Bengt put it, "a first in television commercials." One of the two shots was the obligatory "beauty shot," which is customarily placed at the end of a commercial and shows the product elegantly photographed in an attractive setting. The other shot, the main shot, was to be of a surfer as he is riding and being brought to shore by a giant wave. As the surfboard scrapes the sand at the water's edge, he jumps off and runs up the magnificent beach to a beautiful young woman who is pouring a glassful of this marvelous breakfast food for him. The entire shot of the surfer, from the moment he mounts his surfboard till he takes the glassful of chocolate milk from the smiling beauty, was to be one continuous shot. Bengt's voice was ringing with excitement as he pointed out that this factor alone was going to make this commercial the talk of the industry. As another astonishing fact, he also pointed out that we were going to Hawaii to film the two shots.

I told him I thought it was an interesting concept, but as I was saying that, circuit breakers were popping wildly in my mind. For one thing, I was aware of how precise a television commercial had to be. A one-minute-long commercial meant 60 seconds, not 59 seconds and 12 more frames (being shy of ½ a second), or 60 seconds and six additional frames (representing ¼ of a second). And as the wheels were turning in my mind, I was wondering how we might time the surfer's ride so that it would come out to the exact number of seconds needed before the beauty shot. I pointed out to Bengt that I was not a surfer — in fact, what I didn't know about surfing could fill an encyclopedia — but he didn't think this would matter. He knew, he said, that I would make the images beautiful, and as far as he was concerned that was the important thing. He predicted that this spot was going to win every award for commercials and told me that his company, the ad agency and its client (the food company) were all very high on it. When, after considerable research, he assured the ad agency that this commercial would be as great as he'd described it to me, the agency sold the concept to its client, the food company, who was now looking forward to this very unusual spot as the centerpiece of its next campaign. Bengt also mentioned with some pride that shot for shot, this was going to be the most expensive television commercial ever made. How right that prophecy turned out to be!

But let's take the events step by step in proper chronology. I agreed to go see Bengt the following morning, at which time, he assured me, he would lay out the entire marvelous concept and explain all the details and how we were going to accomplish them. He sounded self-assured, as though he had everything well in hand. I liked him immediately when we met in his office the following morning. Just as his voice suggested on the phone the day before, he turned out to be a pleasant man full of enthusiasm and self-assurance. He started laying out the whole commercial and encouraged me to stop him and ask questions as I felt like it. When he mentioned that the main shot, the surfer surfing to shore on a giant wave, was to last three-quarters of the spot, I asked how we were going to time this. He didn't think this was important because the beauty shot, the product shot, could be adjusted to be longer or shorter, depending on the length of time the surfer took to get to shore. I mentioned that the only thing I knew about surfing was what I occasionally saw on television, but he assured me that even though he also wasn't a surfer, he knew a lot about it, and he asked that I take his word for it. He explained that he had been in touch with two of the world's top surfers, both of who were going to advise us and appear in the commercial. The most important items we would need, which he assumed I knew, would be telephoto lenses. When I brought up the focus problems usually associated with long focal-length lenses, particularly in situations such as working over water, where distance markers could not be used, he told me that the light levels on the beaches in Hawaii were so intense that we could set the lenses to very small iris openings, which would virtually eliminate the problem of focus.

He seemed very knowledgeable about photography and equipment; in fact, he talked about everything in such detail and with such understanding that the more he talked, the more convinced I became that indeed, he did have the situation well in hand. He eloquently described his vision of our opening shot: our surfer on an immense wave, a miniscule, tiny point in the distance, illuminated by the sun behind the wave that was going to make the water sparkle with a "majestic" green luminescence. Bengt was very enthusiastic and very convincing. He further explained that the surfer would know when to start his ride, give or take a couple of seconds, so that getting to the shore would take 45 seconds. He even had figured that our focus problem would be helped by positioning the camera the same distance from the beauty-shot portion of the commercial that the surfer's position was going to be at about the mid-point of his ride. "So you see," he told me with a confident smile, "the focus will hold; the assistant cameraman won't even have to touch the focus knob; we will have no focus problem!" I conceded the point. "This way," he went on, "the surfer won't be too large in the frame as he comes ashore and the size of the shot will be exactly right for the end composition." He told me about the many months of research that went into designing this spot, and pointed out that the ad agency had to be absolutely certain the spot was going to work before it sold the concept to the client and could justify the huge budget necessary to send a crew to a distant and expensive location like Hawaii.

The TV-spot industry, clients and agency people, are known for going to certain locations — Florida in the winter, for example — more for the sake of enjoying it than because of the location's importance to the commercial. I photographed many spots in the glamour places of our planet, suspecting that in some cases it was the agency or its clients who wanted to have a little vacation justified by and charged to the commercial. In one instance, I shot a commercial in January for the Northern Natural Gas Company of Minnesota, advertising natural gas as the fuel of choice for heating one's home. The commercial was filmed in Fort Lauderdale, Florida. As we shot inside a nice, air-conditioned, one-family home, with outside temperatures hovering around 80°, we hung hundreds of dripping plastic icicles from the rain gutters, frosted the windows and spread plastic snow over everything that was visible through the windows — winter attributes that all would have been readily and much more economically available in Minnesota.

But Bengt assured me that this was not the case with our spot. We could have gone to Australia or South Africa, but according to his research, neither of those places had the huge surf the commercial needed. Hawaii was the only place on earth that would give us 60-foot waves. I was not going to argue the point. I didn't know any better, and I wanted to go to Hawaii. Bengt figured we were going to need a couple of days of preparation and a full week to accomplish the work without being pressured.

The trip to Hawaii in the propeller days of air travel, if I recall correctly, took about a full day. By the time we landed we were just about dead, but getting off the plane at Honolulu Airport, with hula girls putting leis around our necks, the sea breeze coming off the ocean and ukulele music coming from speakers, revitalized us, and shortly after checking in at the hotel, all of us met in the dining room for a drink and a late snack. Our group had now swelled to about 12 people: Bengt and his assistants, agency producers, art directors, account executives and, of course, me and my assistant, Tom Priestley.

Bengt's enthusiasm was contagious and spread to all in the group. He told me that the following morning, he was going to fly to Maui to pick up one of our surfers, and because he had to hire a plane large enough for two or three surfboards (which were much larger at that time than they are now), he had extra room and I could come along. Even though it was late and I was tired after the long trip, and going to Maui with Bengt meant getting up early the following day, the opportunity was too good to pass up. It turned out that almost all in our group felt the same way, as the following morning the plane was full. Our surfer was waiting for us at Maui. He seemed small standing next to his surfboards, a modest, young guy just like any typical American college kid. He and his girlfriend wrestled his surfboards into the plane, and within minutes we were in the air again, on our way back to Honolulu.

I suggested to Bengt that as long as we had the plane, we should do a little aerial survey of the area where we were going to work. During my career, I always found aerial reconnaissance helpful; seeing work areas from the air almost always gave me a unique perspective and more often than not revealed information that would not have been available if I had surveyed the same area from the ground. Bengt and just about everyone else aboard was enjoying the magnificent views of the islands and agreed that this was a good idea. I asked our surfer to direct the pilot to where the 60-foot waves were. The young fellow's eyes popped wide open and he asked me to repeat what I'd said, as though he hadn't heard me right. The plane was noisy and I repeated myself, louder this time. He seemed to have a strange smile on his face. "There are no 60-foot waves — not often, that is," he said, smiling. He added with conviction, "And even if there were, very few crazies would dare surf them. I wouldn't." "How big are the waves, then?" I asked him. "Well," he said, "at times we get 30- to 40-footers, and occasionally, three or four days after there is a big storm in Polynesia, we get 60-footers and even some bigger waves, but very few of us ever surf them." He added, "They are very dangerous."

Some within earshot of this conversation fell silent, but the young man, perhaps thinking that he'd said something he shouldn't have, went on. "We have pretty good waves, though — not as big as Australia or South Africa, but the best to surf on. We get longer rides than anywhere in the world." Bengt continued silently looking out the window. "Could you show us where they are?" I asked our surfer. "Sure," he said. "At this time of the year, the best surf is at Haleiwa and the Banzai Pipeline on the North Shore." I felt another red light bulb light up in my head. "Did you say North Shore?" I asked, wondering how to get the sun behind a large wave on the North Shore. "Yeah, you want to see them?" But I thought my curiosity had caused enough problems for one day; I shook my head. Oahu was just ahead, and as far as I was concerned, the aerial survey was a wrap.

But we still had a commercial to shoot. It was early afternoon when we landed at Honolulu and extricated the three surfboards from the plane. Bengt thought that afternoon would be the only time for us to rest up before we started to work the next day, and suggested that we all go our own ways until the following morning. No one suggested meeting for dinner or drinks, so my assistant and I decided to take in the beach right in front of the hotel. It was a pleasant afternoon; the sand was white, the surf calm. There were no 60-foot waves to draw attention away from the many beautiful young women wearing the smallest bikinis.

The following day we went to work. Tommy split off to check out cases and cases of equipment, lots of telephoto lenses, as Bengt, his assistants, the people from the ad agency, our champion surfer, his girlfriend and I went to survey the North Shore of the island. My old Army compass, part of the equipment I always carried on location surveys, indicated that not all was lost. The North Shore of Oahu was actually northwest, more west, in fact, than north, so getting the sun behind a large wave would be possible in the late afternoon. "Golden hour," as we call it in the business, late-afternoon light, just before or just after sunset, was a prime period I always loved for photography, but in this instance I knew it would severely limit the time available to us to make our shot. As I stood there on the beach at Haleiwa, looking at some of the surfers through binoculars, my understanding, perhaps I should say "confusion," about surfing increased, and it became painfully obvious to me that we had another problem— in fact, several other, big problems. Problem number one was that a surfer might be able to ride for 40 or 45 seconds on a ride, though at that time I wasn't able to time anyone for longer than 25 seconds, but it became obvious that we wouldn't be able to keep the surfer on camera for even that length of time because he would disappear behind rising waves between him and us on the beach. Then, as his wave rose and the wave in front of him dipped out of view, he would become visible again, but never where I expected him. As my education about surfing grew, my anxiety also did, and it quickly turned into panic. I became more and more convinced that making the surfer's ride in a single shot was just not going to be possible.

But Bengt had the solution: we would run the camera at higher-than-normal speed, "overcrank it," as we call slow-motion photography, and this would lengthen the shot. As Bengt put it, after some experimentation we would get a full ride. I didn't question him, but by then I knew he was wrong on this and a number of other counts. One, I didn't believe that even overcranking would give us the full ride, and certainly not the end of the ride as the surfer stepped off the board and onto the sand. I also knew that overcranking would make the shot slow-motion, but Bengt thought that this would probably make the shot more interesting. I bowed to his expertise, as commercials were more his business than mine, but reminded him that we still had problem number two: not one surfer rode his or her board all the way to the beach, which is what our storyboards called for. Our surfer was to ride his board onto the sand, jump off and run to meet the beautiful model with a glassful of breakfast goodies. Bengt's enthusiasm never broke. He pointed out with a knowing smile that the surfers we were watching didn't want to come ashore. As soon as the exciting portion of their ride calmed down, they terminated the ride and started looking for the next good wave. Our boy, he said, would ride his board onto the beach. Amen.

But our champion surfer confirmed my fears. "There would be no wave behind the board by then," he explained, "and the board would stop in the shallow, swirling foam, and the surfer would have to jump or fall off." He added, "In most cases, the waves lose their power long before they reach the sand. There is a stretch of water a little farther north where the waves do come ashore, but the shore is rocky and very treacherous." Only the most experienced — or craziest — surfers would surf them occasionally, but every year one or more would drown. Bengt insisted nevertheless that we check out this section, which we did. It was beautiful. The waves were large and dramatic as they broke over the jagged, majestic rock formations rising out of the water. As beautiful as it was, we agreed that the commercial could not be shot here. One after the other, each beach was eliminated, and by late afternoon it became obvious that our chap was right: the best beach for him to surf and for us to shoot the commercial was the first one we visited that morning.

On the way back to the hotel, I looked around in the car. The tired faces of all those curiously silent people indicated that I was not the only one who by this time had grave misgivings about the feasibility of what we had come 5,000 miles to do. I not only had doubts; I was convinced that what we had come to do was, in fact, not possible.

Nevertheless, we were on the beach at Haleiwa bright and early the following morning. Bengt confided that overnight, he figured out a solution to the problem of our surfer disappearing behind the waves. "We have to get the camera high," he told me. Curiously, I'd thought of the same solution but knew that we did not have a crane or a platform, certainly not one that would be high enough; nor did I believe we could come up with one on short notice. I thought of a helicopter, which would have allowed us to track the surfer — in my mind, a much more interesting shot — but even though I didn't say it then, the other difficulties, which kept me awake for the better part of the previous night, seemed insurmountable. Getting the camera on top of even our biggest truck just would not have worked; besides, no cars or other vehicles were permitted on the beach.

Our surfer was on his way once again, paddling his board out in the direction of the endless ocean, looking for the perfect wave. I was watching him through binoculars, ready to start the camera as soon as he looked like he was about to start his ride. Finally he was on his board, heading steeply down the face of a large wave, effortlessly zipping just a few feet in front of the curl chasing him. It was a beautiful shot. Though the sun was not behind the wave, the water had a magnificent (not quite "majestic") luminescence, and I silently thanked Bengt for giving me this opportunity. Then our surfer disappeared behind a rising wave; he was gone! Though I didn't time it, I didn't think the ride was more than 10, maybe 15 seconds long. With film running through the camera at double the normal rate, I desperately searched the top of the waves, trying to find him. When he came into my camera's view again, he was still riding expertly and beautifully, but a few seconds later, another wave in front of him blocked my view and he disappeared again. He kept reappearing and disappearing and then, as he got closer to the beach, he slid off his board and started paddling out to sea again. The next six or seven attempts were equally disappointing and, I knew, unusable. The shot, as far as I was concerned, was a wrap. After we managed to wave him ashore, we broke for lunch.

During lunch, we assessed our situation and decided that a big part of our problem was the lack of communication with our surfer. We had no way of letting him know when he should start his ride, or how to locate him after he dipped out of view. First, we exchanged our surfer's trunks for a green pair with white stripes so he would be easier to spot amongst all the other surfers. We then devised an elaborate signaling system in the form of flags, improvised from our equipment and different-colored shirts and towels, anything we could commandeer from our group, and agreed on the signals telling him we were ready to shoot when he was ready, or not to start a ride (if we were reloading the camera, changing a lens, or for any other reason were not ready to shoot). I hoped he would remember the signals; I knew I wouldn't, but I wasn't handling the flags, and Bengt seemed to have the situation, once again, well in hand. As it turned out, the signals were understood, but they didn't help much. By sunset we had shot more than our daily allotment of raw stock (film) but still didn't have anything like the "single, 45-second-long continuous shot" we came to get. We put cold cream on our newly acquired sunburns and called it a wrap. The first day was over and, wisely, Bengt decided not to send the exposed film to the lab in case we did get the perfect take the following day (which would make all takes from the previous day superfluous).

But the next four days were equally unproductive, I could say disastrous. We did get the beauty shot portion of our commercial during a time when the surf was down, but the problem was that unless we had the shot leading up to the beauty shot, by itself the beauty shot would be of no value. In other words, we had a very nice ending to a commercial that didn't exist — one that, in my opinion, we would not get. Bengt decided not to work on the weekend. It would be too expensive, and furthermore, there would be too many people on the beach and in the water to try to work around.

As an active pilot, I decided to rent a small plane and take my assistant, Tommy, and an agency producer for a ride around the islands. The flight was beautiful. From up high, we could see the shadows of the yachts on the ocean floor through the crystal-clear water. The color of the coral ranged from black to deep blue, light blue and green, and to various shades of red, orange, yellow and purple. We flew over the cliffs where, according to Hawaiian legend, thousands of warriors jumped to their deaths for some reason I no longer remember, and over vast pineapple plantations, dense jungle and magnificent waterfalls. On the way back to Honolulu, I traced the route the Japanese aircraft took over Hickam Field on their way to Pearl Harbor on December 7, 1941. The rest of the weekend was equally pleasant. I went sightseeing, did some shopping like most of the tourists, and had a marvelous Japanese dinner.

Over the weekend — I am guessing, of course — there must have been some interesting meetings and telephone calls about cost overruns, and how, or if, we were going to get the footage we still needed. I managed a brief meeting with Bengt, but he was still so overly certain we would get the shot that I didn't press and didn't go beyond expressing a mild doubt.

Monday morning came and, hoping for the best, we rolled out again, ready to give it another try. But having been in the business for some time by then, I hadn't seen too many situations where a seemingly impossible shot miraculously worked out, and in this case, I knew nothing short of a miracle would help our situation. But a miracle we did not get! We shot a lot of film, none of which came even close to the original concept of the commercial. I knew the only way we had a chance of possibly getting the shot — though no guarantee could be given for the length of the shot, or that the surfer would be able to go all the way to the water's edge — was from a helicopter. But for reasons unknown to me, my idea was promptly rejected.

A one-minute television spot is exactly 90 feet of film. By the end of the second week, we had shot close to 15,000 feet of film. Fortunately, none of it was sent to the lab for processing, as we knew there was nothing on film even remotely resembling a 45-second ride all the way to the beach. Our champion surfer had to go back to school on Maui, and even though we had the number-two-ranked surfer as a replacement, he held out no great promise, given that we had failed with number one. In fairness, it must be said that the surfers' abilities were not responsible for our failure.

Both performed at a world-class, championship level but could not tailor their abilities to conform to the design and requirements of an ill-conceived television commercial. It was obvious that if we wanted to go home with anything usable, we had to redesign the commercial to fit the realities.

Bengt sent the exposed negative in for processing so we could see what we had and what we would have to shoot in the next couple of days in order to assemble a usable spot. When we looked at the footage at a local movie theater around midnight, after the last showing, most of the 15,000 feet was disappointing. There were interesting, well executed shots amongst the thousands of feet of short takes, including footage of other surfers wearing green trunks with white stripes, but we didn't have a single take as it was conceived for the commercial. We had some exciting and spectacular wipe-outs, and we even had some gorgeous shots of huge, luminescent waves and beautiful rides through the Banzai Pipeline, but no single shot even came close to 45 seconds or ended with the surfer jumping off his board at the water's edge and running up to the beautiful model.

The screening was followed by an intense meeting that ended at close to 5 o'clock in the morning, and after many suggestions, it was decided that we would continue to try for two more days, during which time we would also concentrate on getting additional shots that, when connected with short dissolves, would convey the feeling of one continuous ride. I no longer remember who made this suggestion, but I distinctly remember that nobody really bought it. The next day — I should say later the same day — most of the agency people left for New York. They promised to look at what we had when we came back to New York and, if the spot was good enough, to go back to their client with a new proposal. Bengt, his assistants, my assistant and I stayed for another week. We shot a lot of footage with a young local surfer when our number-two champion also had to return to school. This young fellow turned in the best performances yet, though he admittedly was not as good a surfer as the other two. He did things the other two would not, including riding his board close enough to the beach that he could jump off and run up the beach. Unfortunately, his board broke or was somehow damaged during that ride, but we did have him on film running up the beach toward a replacement blond model who looked very much like the first one. On Friday, the last day of our shoot, as we were having a wonderful catered lunch on the beach, Bengt told me the new commercial was going to be much better than the original two-shot commercial would have been. The long take of the two-shot commercial, he said, would not have sustained audience interest for the better part of a minute; it would have been boring, dull and uninteresting. With all the new and interesting footage we now had, he would have no problem cutting a super spot, and if the agency didn't like it, he was going to take the spot right to the client.

We had a wonderful three weeks in Hawaii and, referring to the work, Bengt said that none of it was wasted. Though I appreciated his compliments, they didn't make me feel any better about not getting what we came to get. Shortly after lunch, Hawaii, and possibly the most expensive commercial second for second, was a wrap.

I never saw the commercial on the air, and I suspect it never made it. Likewise, and regretfully, I haven't seen or heard from Bengt since, nor have I heard from anyone who has.

Looking back on this experience, I still find being part of spending a vast amount of money on a hopeless project regrettable. The era during which this particular experience took place is remembered as the heyday of television-commercial production, and the stories of excesses are endless. But I think the "60-Foot-High Wave" commercial must be amongst the contenders for top honors.

There have been many instances, even in my own career, of well-planned, high-budget films or expensive portions of films that never saw the light of day. But there were also instances when unplanned, extremely valuable pluses came our way unexpectedly. Such was the case a few years later, when I was shooting a movie in Africa. Well, why don't I tell you the whole story in the next chapter?

NIGERIA

Perhaps because our car was the newest, or because we had the best driver, Ossie Davis and I were once again the first ones to arrive at the location of our day's work. It was still early. The morning ground fog that is so characteristic to this region of Africa still hugged the ground, and the warm, orange rays of the rising sun were just beginning to clip the tops of the tall hardwood trees. We knew we had some time before the rest of our company and equipment arrived, and as usual, this was the best time for the two of us to once again go over the day's work and lay out any changes that may have been born the night before. By that time, we had been in Nigeria for some weeks, shooting the feature film *Countdown at Kusini* (1976), which Ossie was directing as well as acting in with his wife, Ruby Dee. The movie depicts the struggles of an African statesman dedicated to the liberation of his country and his people from colonial rule. The film's hero, Motapo, is played by Ossie. He and I first met some years before in New York while working on the television movie *Teacher, Teacher*, in which Ossie also starred. We have been friends ever since.

The village we came to that morning was still quiet and seemed almost deserted, as early morning was the best time to sleep in the bush. It was cool and peaceful. An occasional rooster announced the start of another day, another workday for Ossie and me. Our location scouts carefully picked this village, and indeed, it was ideal for our purposes. The scene we were to shoot that day depicted Motapo arriving by river at this rural village after winning a battle with mercenaries. The river flowed slowly by the village with the jungle of the rainforest along its graceful turns. In the scene, Motapo comes ashore with the soldiers of his ragtag army, and the

Director/actor Ossie Davis, me and camera operator Howard Block (by camera).

village elders (played by professional Nigerian actors) welcome him.

The village was a typical West African village, pleasantly situated along the banks of the river. There were large trees along the banks and a good-sized clearing with an old oil press where the women of the village pressed oil from a variety of nuts at the right times in the seasons. Some of the ever-present, scrawny dogs, chickens and goats looked us over from behind makeshift fences along the huts of the village as we sat on a log alongside our car. The morning breeze wafted a strange but melodious chanting to us from the direction of some distant huts. The singing was pretty, yet sad somehow. After listening to it for a bit, Ossie and I decided to investigate. We walked through the village, drawn by the strange quality of the sounds, as around us the village was waking up, coming slowly to life. More and more people appeared from the huts. Some threw curious glances at us; others smiled and waved a friendly gesture of greeting. Many of them were heading in the direction of the chanting, and as it got louder, we came upon a group sitting on chairs, benches and upturned buckets, drinking what appeared to be beer. A smaller group was chanting. As soon as they saw us, some got up, offering us their chairs, and one of the women offered us beer. This was a bit early to start drinking, but as I found out later, drinking beer was a tradition at funerals. This was the funeral of a young man, but there was no coffin or anything else that would have suggested a funeral. More people were arriving. They were also offered beer, but it soon occurred to me that nobody sat down after we sat. They just sort of grouped around Ossie, who was wearing his camouflage fatigues, his costume for the movie. Ossie, a big man, is an impressive, imposing figure, and even as he sat there quietly, the group of villagers, which was now about 50 people, sensed his authority and importance. At about that time, our crew and cast buses began pulling in, followed by equipment trucks and personal cars. Actors dressed as soldiers, weapons and all, as well as other actors dressed as village elders and dignitaries were getting off the buses. Ossie and I stood up, ready to join our group. The mourners bowed to us and offered silent handshakes and more beer, but we left to start our day's work.

~ ~ ~

Let me stop and deviate a bit and give you a little background on our project, how it came about and how our experience in Africa was shaping up by that time. Like most projects, *Countdown at Kusini* started with a telephone call. A producer I had not heard of before wanted to know the usual: was I available, could I come into Manhattan to discuss a project, and could I go to Africa the following day? My wife was sitting under the hairdryer at the hairdressers when I called her about going to Africa the following day. She knew it wasn't a flip wisecrack; this sort of thing had happened before, and she agreed to come home right away to get my passport and help me pack.

Ossie Davis, the film's star and director, was at the producer's office in New York City by the time I got there. His producer explained that the cinematographer who was to shoot the film had backed out, and they needed to know if I would be willing to take his place on such short notice. That sort of thing was never an easy decision, particularly when the film was independently produced by mostly unknown people. But I knew Ossie and agreed to read the script that night, pick a camera crew and be ready to leave in two days. I had nothing else on the horizon; I had never been to Africa, and Africa beckoned.

The trip to Lagos was full of unusual experiences, but in view of larger things, I won't waste time talking about them. I will cut to the more important elements of this story because I know that if I decided to write about nothing else but this film, it could fill a volume, possibly two.

It is important that you understand first and foremost that nothing, absolutely nothing, worked in Nigeria at that time. The foul-ups were endless, and the things that went wrong or simply did not happen while we were trying to film *Countdown at Kusini* formed a never-ending chain of unexpected, at times unbelievable, events. I'll just mention a few. As there was nothing to do after work in Lagos, the capital of Nigeria, nowhere to go in the evening, the crew usually congregated in the so-called Rose Garden of the Ikoyi Hotel to sip beer and swap the disaster stories of the day. Not all of the stories related to making the movie. Some were personal experiences, and it would be impossible to list all or even most of the memorable ones, but I will mention a few simply to help you understand and appreciate what is to come.

Our script supervisor ordered room-service breakfast one morning: two eggs, bacon, juice, toast and coffee. She got a tray of 16 empty dessert dishes and half a roasted chicken. She had no breakfast that morning, but all of us had something to laugh about that evening as we tried to come up with a reasonable explanation for some of the many strange things that went wrong that day — or any other day.

Most of us rolled out early the first morning in Lagos and eagerly waited for the cars to take us location-scouting. The cars, incidentally, were provided by the Nigerian government and were supposed to arrive at 7, but when there was no sign of them an hour later, our nervous production manager went to telephone our contact to find out where the cars were. He was informed, he told us later, that the government motor pool usually did not open till later in the morning, sometimes as late as 9 o'clock, but his contact promised to inform the dispatcher to open the motor pool earlier than usual for our cars. The next morning, we were once again hanging around in front of the hotel at 7, but the cars weren't there. At around 9 o'clock, the cars arrived, and the drivers told our production manager that the motor pool had opened at half past 6, per our request, but the petrol (gas) pumps didn't dispense gas until later in the morning. There was no set time for petrol dispensation; it happened, we were told, as the situation required, sometimes in the morning, sometimes in the afternoon, sometimes not at all. Some more telephone calls between the right parties got this situation under control, and our cars were to be gassed up the night before from then on.

We should have learned from this and similar incidents, but there were so many of them and they were so unexpected and illogical that no lessons could be learned. Even though we were working in Africa, the American crewmembers were under American union contracts with specific conditions, such as lunch being called no more that five hours after the start of the day's work. This meant we had to break for lunch by noon, but the dining room in the hotel (the only relatively safe place to eat) did not open till 12:30. Going to lunch at 12:30 meant a half hour of uncalled-for and expensive overtime, and the production department therefore persuaded the hotel management to open the restaurant for the film crew a half-hour ahead of the regular time. The next day, the doors of the restaurant opened precisely at 12, but soon after we got seated it became obvious that there wasn't a waiter in sight. Further investigation revealed that while the hotel management granted our wish and opened the dining room early, no arrangements had been made to serve food earlier than usual because no such request was made. We were beginning to learn our lessons — we thought — and went ahead with our work as best as possible.

We needed a classy outdoor restaurant for a lunch scene, but our location scouts could not come up with one; they told us there was no such thing in Lagos. Ossie and I, accompanied by some of our key people, went to look for something that could take the restaurant's place. In the center of the city, just behind one of the large office buildings, was a good-sized cement deck surrounded by a few trees. From the looks of it, it had not been used for anything lately, if ever. It was dirty, with garbage blowing around in the wind, but oddly enough, off to one side was what looked like a very nice little fountain. I thought that with very little effort, we could turn this deck into a terrace restaurant. Rows of stands with flowers would fence in the restaurant, and with enough high-end restaurant paraphernalia, uniformed waiters and well-dressed clientele, this would be exactly what our story and the script called for. When I asked about the fountain, I was told that I would have to talk with the building's chief engineer. One of our production assistants went to fetch him, and when he showed up, he turned out to be a very nice, cooperative fellow. I asked him if he could turn the fountain on for us on the day of the filming, and he assured me that he would. I was mentally registering some camera angles through the spray and cascade of water, making camera moves that would incorporate and pay off this unexpected, elegant little bonus to its best advantage.

When we arrived at the restaurant set some weeks after first seeing the site, even I was surprised at how well it now suited the requirements of the story. It looked great. Our art director and his crew did a great job. Looking at it, one would not have thought that it was not a real restaurant. Our art director even parked some expensive cars around the perimeter of the terrace, and the elegantly dressed maitre d' and waiters and the actors at the tables looked like the highest echelon of this fictitious African city's elite. We rehearsed the scene, and the time came to make the first shot. I sent a production assistant to tell the chief engineer to turn on the fountain. A few minutes later, the engineer came to see me. "The fountain is on, sir," he said. At first, I thought it might take a few minutes to build up pressure before the water would come on, but after a minute or so, when nothing happened, I asked, "Where is the water?"

Director/actor Ossie Davis, me and camera operator Howard Block (by camera).

"Ahh, water," the chief engineer sighed. "There is no water, sir." I didn't think I heard right, but he explained that when the building was built, somebody forgot to install the water pipes for the fountain, and by the time this oversight was discovered, the cement had been poured, so the pipes were never installed. The building engineer, cooperative fellow that he was, turned on the pump for me, but....

Had I known this ahead of time, we could have installed our own pump and supply of water. But now, all I could do was tell the set dressers to buy some potted plants and turn the fountain into a very large flower stand. I tried not to include it in too many of the shots and thought I'd learned another lesson that I hoped would help me get through the picture.

The script called for aerial footage of a small railroad station in the bush being strafed by a vintage warplane. We found an ideal little station in the forest, and the railroad officials promised us a train at the right time. I was also told that the Nigerian air force would loan us a vintage plane to do the strafing and a helicopter to film the action from. But every time I asked to see the plane and the helicopter, my request was stonewalled — ignored might be a better word — and I never did get to see either aircraft. It was time to bring this to Ossie's attention, as by then I was convinced that neither the vintage plane nor the helicopter was going to materialize. The closest place we could bring a helicopter from was France or Italy, but the company didn't have that in the film's budget. The only alternative was to cut the strafing scene out of the script or perhaps replace it with a ground attack. All of us were sorry we might have to let go of the strafing scene. It was an exciting part of the movie, but there seemed to be no way to film it.

I took matters in hand and found out there was a local flying club at a small airport just outside Lagos. The airport's name was Kiri-Kiri and the flying club was known as, you guessed it, the Kiri-Kiri Flying Club. One of my local assistants, who by this time had become a friend, volunteered to take me to Kiri-Kiri the following weekend. Not surprisingly, the airport was a relatively level piece of grass pasture with a few cows, and the "club" was a wooden shack that had seen better days. There were four, maybe five small planes, single-engine Cessnas and Pipers, all needing a new paint job and probably other repairs. One of these planes, a Cessna 182, belonged, I was told, to a Dutch man. We found a telephone number for him, and he agreed to meet me the following weekend. He turned out to be a nice, young fellow who used the plane for pleasure and some sort of business he didn't talk about. What he did tell me was that there were three civilian airports in Nigeria: Lagos International Airport, the International Airport at Ibadan, and Kiri-Kiri. There were a few other strips he knew of and would occasionally fly to, but he pointed out that only Lagos International and Ibadan sold petrol. Kiri-Kiri had a petrol pump but only dispensed gas now and then. Because of this situation, my Dutch friend told me, he installed long-range tanks in his plane, allowing him three times the range and peace of mind because he knew he could always reach one of the three airports. After he found out I was a fellow pilot, he graciously agreed to let me use his plane for the filming. This was the best (and only) game in town.

The strafing scene was back in the script, though altered to suit the type of plane we had. Instead of strafing, Col. Ben Ahmed, Motapo's mercenary adversary, was going to buzz the station, perhaps to reconnoiter it, or for some other reason a mercenary colonel in the service of his colonial masters might have. Perhaps out of habit, or to make ourselves feel better, we continued to refer to the scene as the "strafing scene." The problem was that no maps like the aviation maps in the United States were available for flying in Nigeria. Ordinary, gas-station-variety roadmaps showed the highways — more or less — but once one got away from the Lagos area, there was nothing under the plane but endless jungle. My newly found Dutch friend recommended that I take along a young local kid, his friend, who, my Dutch friend explained, flew with him often and knew the area well from the air. When it turned out that this kid knew where the railroad station was that we were supposed to strafe, it was like having a guide and a trustworthy navigation system aboard. The kid was an enthusiastic flyer who was hoping to become a pilot someday. He was waiting for us at the plane early on the morning we were going to do the strafing shots. I gave the plane a walk-around inspection and, as expected, nothing worked the way it should have. If we had been in the United States, I would have called a junk dealer, but in Nigeria this was the only thing available. I was itching to go, to salvage the "strafing scene," and anxious to do a little flying, my favorite pastime. The adrenaline was flowing. The plane, I was told, had just come back from a long trip up north, so it was reasonable to believe that it was in flying condition. Besides, I told myself, I'd turn around at the first sign of trouble and head back to the airport. In fact, I was planning to do a few tests within gliding distance of the airport before we set out for the railroad station. A manual check of the controls assured me that they all worked, but some of the instruments did not. That didn't bother me too much, as by then I knew that there weren't any radio navigation aids this plane was equipped with that worked in Nigeria. One VOR station (one of the simpler forms of navigation aids) was erected at Lagos International a few years prior to this incident, but, as I was told, the technician who activated it accidentally backed his truck into the antenna and smashed it, and the VOR transmitter never came on line.

What did bother me was that there was no way of telling how much gas we had in the gas tanks. The gas gauges were both broken, but my young guide told me the long-range tanks had petrol. An improvised dipstick could not negotiate the elbow in the fill pipe, but when I looked into the tanks on the top of the wing, there seemed to be gas in both. So, with all that in mind, I put Tom Aldredge, the actor playing the ex-French Foreign Legion officer Col. Ben Ahmed, head of the mercenary army, into the left rear seat, and my camera operator, Howard Block, next to him with a small handheld camera, a back-up battery for the camera and three rolls of film. I got into the plane, my young guide settled into the front passenger seat, and after I made sure that the doors were securely locked, I turned the key in the ignition. To my great surprise, the engine fired up easily and purred reassuringly, and the controls and the engine checked out faultlessly as we started to taxi. There were no runways; one could take off in any direction the wind came from, so we did. The plane flew surprisingly well and was very quiet. The weather was ideal and the air was smooth in the early morning. I made a few test turns — revved up the engine and pulled the power, worked the flaps, did a few stalls — and was pleased that everything but the radio worked well. I tried several international frequencies for Lagos International Airport but received no answer.

The country was beautiful from high up in the early morning as I headed for the railroad tracks in the bush that would lead us to the station. We flew over small villages where kids chased the plane, and soon we found the railroad tracks. We tried our own walkie-talkie-type radios, and they worked. As I circled the railroad station, I could see our people and cameras in position to shoot us as we buzzed the station. It seemed that Ossie's ragtag army and everything else was ready for the shoot. We made several practice runs and necessary adjustments, and within a short time were ready to shoot the scene. Every run we made was perfect. By about 11 or so, the scripted shots were "in the can;" our mission was accomplished, and I suggested some other shots: flying directly at the ground-based camera, making low passes that tied the plane in with the station building and foreground action, everything we could think of to use the plane to the best advantage. There is an expression for this in the movie business: "milking it." It means exploiting an opportunity. Howard, in the back seat, was out of film, but we had more good footage than we needed, and as there was no other work scheduled for the day, it was time to head home.

Though I knew how hot it must have been on the ground, the plane was comfortably cool, and with the rest of the day open, all of us in the plane agreed to do a little aerial sightseeing. The movie business allows these occasional perks, and we were about to take advantage of it. My young guide did know the area well and directed us from one interesting sight to another, but as the air warmed up and the plane started to bounce, I decided it was time to head for Kiri-Kiri. The city of Lagos, with Kiri-Kiri at its far edge, was dead ahead. I climbed up to 5,000 feet. Lagos sprawled below us, a huge city with a modern inner core of large glass-and-steel office buildings that was surrounded by endless shantytowns of corrugated sheet-metal roofs supported by thin stilts, all of it teeming with humanity. Then the engine coughed — just once at first, but almost immediately a couple of more times. Though I didn't think this would be possible with the high temperatures, it sounded like ice could be forming in the carburetor. My hands automatically went for the red Carbheat knob and pulled it "on" and, indeed, the engine settled down. But just a few seconds later, the engine coughed again, backfired and caught again. This wasn't carburetor ice. Instinctively, I looked at the gas gauges, realizing immediately that they were of no use. There was nothing else I could think of: we were running out of gas. I eased back on the throttle and pushed the nose down a bit, hoping that even if we did run out of gas, we could glide back to Kiri-Kiri. As I was now flying at the lowest throttle setting, trying to conserve fuel, the plane was bumping along, and the stall-warning horn came on now and then as we hit some of the warm updrafts over the city. Unconsciously, I was looking for a clearing ahead, just in case, but the only thing below us was the endless shantytown that surrounds Lagos. I trimmed up the plane and hung onto the yoke, trying to get the most out of the plane's glide. I suspected — actually, I was pretty well convinced — that we were running out of gas. The endless shantytown rolled agonizingly slowly below us, but we didn't seem to get any closer to the edge of the city and Kiri-Kiri beyond it. The stall-warning horn was now blaring almost continuously. "What is that noise?" Howard asked. I gave some cockamamie explanation and wondered how he could even consider believing it. My young guide, who apparently knew what the stall-warning horn was about, seemed pale even though he was a native of Nigeria, and sat motionless, staring straight ahead, as though paralyzed. The ground was coming up at us. Now and then I tried the throttle and the plane perked up a bit, but when the nose came up it would cough again, and I went back to the glide. I added a little power as Kiri-Kiri came into what I judged to be gliding distance, and minutes later the plane settled onto a grass field. We hardly rolled at all before the engine coughed and died. "That was a beautiful landing," Howard complimented me, and I wondered if he was serious or sarcastic. But we were on the ground, and we pushed the plane to the petrol pump, hoping that it was operating. Aside from giving thanks for being alive, I was pleased to have saved the strafing sequence and hoped that none of my passengers suspected how close they might have come to the end of their respective careers.

The funeral chants were still coming from the distance as Ossie and I picked camera positions for our scenes. We were assured that by the time we were ready to film, the funeral would be over, but even if it wasn't it would be all right for us to do our work. Life in the village, we were told, would go on as usual. We found a particularly nice spot at the river's edge, near a clearing that had the village in the background, where Motapo could come ashore and be greeted by actors playing village elders and dignitaries. We blocked

Funeral chanters with drums.

the action while assistant directors arranged the background action of the small boats arriving from around a bend in the river. Motapo was to be in the lead boat, surrounded by his soldiers. Some other soldiers, already ashore and in the village, were jubilantly celebrating, firing their weapons in victory celebration as Motapo came ashore and met the villagers.

Just about this time, drumming started somewhere in the village. I recognized the sing-song wailing of the Yoruba talking drums, and shortly we also heard similar drumming starting up in the distance. We had no idea what the drumming was about; I thought it was part of the funeral, and our sound engineer, delighted at this extra flavor, had his recorders going. All of us hoped the drumming would continue during the filming, as it was a truly great and authentic local touch. As we were getting the scene shot by shot, singing started somewhere in the village just as Ossie was being filmed coming ashore and into the village. The singing was beautiful. Those who have never heard real African singing can have no idea how beautiful it is. The melodies were mellow and harmonious.

It played a come-and-go game with the funeral chanting that was still going on but became stronger and stronger, finally drowning out the funeral chants. Then I saw dancers in colorful costumes coming toward us from between the huts. I yelled to Howard, my A-camera operator, to roll and get as much of this as possible. Our Nigerian camera operators also took the cue and switched on their cameras. I knew this was not part of our plan and frankly didn't care, as long as I could get some of it on film. It was interesting and beautiful, and I hoped it could somehow become part of the movie. I grabbed a small handheld camera and ran toward the dancers. I shot close-up after close-up of the dancing; smiling, joyful faces in the crowd; colorful, swirling skirts and bare feet; jewelry, and, the biggest plus of all, sleeping babies in sacks on their dancing mothers' backs. The wheels were turning rapidly in my head. All this wonderful, totally unexpected footage, my brain told me, could become the best part of the celebration scene of Motapo's jubilant entry into the village. I didn't even care if the other cameras photographed me, because in such a celebration, I reasoned, I could have been a newsreel cameraman on the spot. The dancers were coming closer and it was becoming clear that indeed, though not planned, they were part of the celebration.

This was a spontaneous expression celebrating an unannounced event. And unlike our make-believe ceremony of "village elders" greeting Motapo, this was real. Within minutes, the dancers were in front of Ossie and his soldiers. The singing went on as the dancers formed a circle around Ossie, who was also enjoying this unannounced happening. He waved to the crowd and went on acting the role of a conquering hero to the hilt. A group of men, real villagers, had Ossie on their shoulders and were dancing with him to the melodies of the singing and the beat of the drums. It didn't seem that the dancing would ever stop. When it finally did, Ossie was seated on a bench atop the mound where the oil press was, surrounded by a real, adoring crowd of villagers. We had a quick "council of war" as to what else to shoot in order to be able to use all the wonderful footage that had just fallen into our laps. With the help of interpreters, we arranged to shoot some bridging cuts, and we finished the filming with this added plus, which we filmmakers like to call "added production value." I thanked God for our good fortune to be in the village during this celebration. We still didn't fully understand the reason for all the dancing and singing but really didn't care, as long as we had all this marvelous footage as part of our scene. It was a huge dose of unexpected "added production value." Ossie and I were delighted, and the two of us couldn't stop speculating about our good fortune all the way back to Lagos and the Ikoyi Hotel.

It turned out that all of us were similarly affected. When we met in the Rose Garden after dinner for our nightly swap of "Nigeria stories," instead of the usual foul-ups, the conversation centered on our good fortune at being able to film the village festival. Then somebody casually mentioned that for some reason or the other, more than a few of our local crew had left the shoot, some even before the dancing began. By then, that sort of thing — crewmembers leaving the shoot without telling anyone — was not new. It had happened before and was not something we spent too much time wondering about, but that night, as the melodies were still echoing in my head and I was unable to go to sleep, a foreboding feeling crept into my mind. Did our Nigerian crewmembers leave the shoot, I asked myself, because they were afraid of something? Did they know something the American contingent didn't know? And if they did, what was it? I kept speculating.

At that time, Nigeria was a military dictatorship. The present government had taken over from a previous military dictatorship, as so many other governments of that country had in the past. These dictatorships lasted for varying lengths of time; some went on for years, while others would come and go within weeks. Indeed, shortly after we left Nigeria, the government that was in power while we were there was toppled and replaced by another military coup. I recalled that the drums started as Motapo's army was coming ashore and his soldiers were firing their guns in celebration. Could it be that the Yoruba members of our crew understood the drums to be news of a military takeover that was going out over the jungle network of drums?

Even today, when I recall this, I shudder to think of what might have happened if, indeed, the drums were sending out messages about a group of revolutionaries, boatloads of soldiers and their commander taking over the village and celebrating victory. What would have happened if those drum messages were understood by or brought to the attention of someone in the real Nigerian military? I won't even speculate about the possibilities. I do know that if something like that had happened, filming in Nigeria for us would have been a wrap — a major wrap!

The drums in Nigeria, and in some other parts of Africa, do talk. Many of us remember the movie *Stanley and Livingston*, one of many films about Africa, and speculate as to whether drums could really carry a message, as those movies claimed. I found out that they could. The Yoruba talking drum, unlike the large, hollowed-out tree-trunk drums of *Stanley and Livingston*, is a small, ornate drum that hangs from a strap on its owner's shoulder. Out of curiosity, while we were working in the bush, I asked one of the people who had one to send a message to one of my nearby camera crew. The message did get through and was confirmed by walkie-talkie radio.

The Yoruba drums are played with a curved stick that has a leather-clad head. The way they work, it was explained to me, is that the operator, using his elbow, applies pressure to the leather tongs of the drum to tighten or relax the drum heads, the skin of the drums, which emit a different sound depending on the tension, imitating the inflictions and intonations of the Yoruba language. A very nicely made specimen of a Yoruba talking drum, one of my prized possessions, still hangs on my den wall. At times I demonstrate how it works to friends, but I am never sure if the message gets through. I suspect some things get lost in the translation. Yoruba is a very difficult language!

REAL COPS, REAL BULLETS,
EXPLOSIONS AND GARBAGE

Not all unexpected incidents are bonuses for a film. The real bullets that the Nigerian military most probably would have fired at us as we filmed Ossie Davis' victory celebration in the African village, bullets that could have killed us, almost did just that to an unsuspecting actor on another project.

Let's start at the beginning.

Real bullets have no place in filmmaking, yet at times, as in the case of my experience in Africa, the danger of facing them can be all too real. Shooting a scene where bullets are seen hitting a person or an object is really a very simple matter. Case in point: the *Shōgun* scene I described, in which Toronaga runs a blockade of fishing boats, illustrates how simple it is to simulate bullet hits using squibs, small, electronically detonated explosive charges. Unlike the weapons used in that film, all firearms used in films depend on blank charges when guns are seen blazing away. Even the U.S. military uses blanks on training exercises, but I doubt that the Nigerian military would have considered using blanks had they believed that the army of liberation led by Ossie Davis that landed in the jungle village was part of a military takeover of the country.

On another film, *Love Is Forever*, filmed in Thailand, we had the full cooperation of the Thai government, and a large unit of the Thai army was placed at our disposal. This was a tremendous plus, as the film called for large army units, at times furiously firing their weapons. One such occasion came as we were filming on the Mekong River in northern Thailand. The scene called for our hero — for the sake of brevity, I won't describe the whole plot — to swim underwater from one side of the Mekong to the other, occasionally coming to the surface for air. The patrol boats were to drop hand grenades as soldiers shot real bullets into the river where, according to the story, our swimmer hero was believed to be. The soldiers had carte blanche with the ammunition and were having the time of their lives blasting away at an imaginary enemy under the water. Bullets were flying everywhere. For the purpose of my photography, the profusion and the effect of bullets hitting the water could not have been better. It was superior to anything our meager special-effects department could have created on the spot, but I was scared out of my wits, as were most of our cast and crew.

Fortunately, nobody was hurt. We managed to kill a bunch of fish, which turned out to be a boon to some villagers downriver, as the surface of the water was covered with fish stunned or killed by the concussion of hand grenades. This incident was a rare example of using real firearms and real bullets in connection with film production. In most places, this would be a violation of laws restricting or specifically forbidding the use of real ammunition for filming a movie. And of course, we assured ourselves that we were in total control and that all necessary safety considerations had been taken. Unfortunately, there were a few occasions in my years of making movies when we were not in total — or, for that matter, any degree — of control.

One such incident happened early one morning in the Bronx, one of New York City's northern boroughs, while we were preparing to make a shot for a very popular television show of the Sixties, *Naked City*. But before I go into what happened that morning, let me tell you a bit about this show for the benefit of those who may not remember it, or are too young to have ever seen it. *Naked City* was about three New York police detectives, played by Paul Burke, Harry Bellaver and Horace McMahon. The segments of the weekly one-hour show were filmed in studios in New York and on location around the city. In fact, the city became as much a star of this series as the cast was. Audiences outside New York enjoyed watching the show to see the city's landmark sites as much as to see the stars of the show. In that respect, *Naked City* was a forerunner of other television shows and feature films that use New York City locations extensively even today, instead of filming more conveniently and economically on sound stages and back lots.

Filming on location was always more difficult than filming in the studio, but it added a quality of realism that studio-filmed shows generally did not have. Good weather or bad, we filmed at interesting locations in New York City; its elevated trains, concert halls, garbage dumps, wide avenues, narrow alleys, parks, skyscrapers and tenements all became our "back lot." Because filming on New York streets was not as commonplace at that time as it is today, in order not to attract crowds we tried to film with hidden or at least somewhat camouflaged cameras whenever possible. At times we would put the camera into a panel truck or cover it with a tarpaulin to avoid attracting attention. There were times when such camouflaging was not possible, and at those times the New York Police Department would close the street, direct traffic around and away from us, and help with crowd control. Even with all that help, filming on New York streets was never easy. There

Setting up an action stunt for *Naked City* with coordinator Max Kleven.

would be "fender-bender" car accidents as passing drivers, distracted by the filming, bumped into each other. At other times, kids would jump in front of the camera during filming, mugging, waving and yelling, "Take my picture, mister!"

I recall one incident that occurred as we were setting up to film a car crash. I no longer remember the storyline, nor is it important, but I recall that the scene called for two police cars to turn onto

Shooting a fight scene above the streets of New York City, for *Naked City*.

a Lower East Side street going the wrong way, against the traffic, and crash into a black sedan coming from the opposite direction. That was the action. We blocked it, placed the cameras and went through the action in slow motion, rehearsing the scene for the cameras and the stunt drivers. By this time, a large crowd had gathered behind police barricades to watch us film. Because stunts and crashes can be unpredictable and dangerous even with the most thorough planning, they are usually filmed with multiple cameras covering all the angles to ensure getting all the action even if one of the cameras should malfunction. Multiple cameras are also needed because in such a scene, the vehicles are often damaged and retakes are not possible. All camera crews know to stop a stunt when something goes wrong; if, let's say, there is a problem with a camera, the stunt action can be halted before damage is done and set up again after the problem with the camera is fixed. Stopping a stunt has to happen quickly and decisively.

That morning, as we stood poised to film this crash after all preparations were made, the command to "roll 'em" came, and the camera operators flipped the switches on their cameras. Looking intently through the cameras' viewfinders, one by one they gave the traditional acknowledgement of being ready, calling out loud and clear: "Camera one, speed," "Camera two, speed," and "Camera three, speed." "Speed" — motion-picture lingo — simply means that a camera is running smoothly and the operator is ready to film the action. The expression dates back to the early days of sound movies, when a camera had to run at a certain speed in order to be synchronized with the sound-recording equipment. As the cameras were running, stunt drivers were revving their engines, waiting for the action cue. The crowds hushed as the cue came, and the "police" cars came barreling down Second Avenue, ready to turn onto the side street and crash into the black sedan. As the crash became imminent, a loud and urgent "Cut! CUT! CUUUT!!" was heard. Reacting to this command, the camera operators, having been conditioned by years of training, automatically reached for the camera switches and shut the cameras down. A second or so later, the cars crashed. The stunt drivers did their job well. When the cloud of steam from the burst radiators lifted, we saw three cars piled into one gigantic mess, their front ends buckled, smashed sheet metal. A stunned bunch of filmmakers, three confused and embarrassed camera operators, were looking around, trying to figure out who called "Cut." There was no doubt in anyone's mind that somebody did; in fact, when the sound tape was played back, the voice yelling, "Cut! CUT!" was heard loud and clear. But trying to find out who yelled it at that point was meaningless. We had three cars smashed beyond recognition and repair and no footage to show for it. (Later, when we speculated about what had happened, we imagined the voice could have come from a rooftop or a nearby window, or from some clown in the crowd who got carried away with his familiarity with motion-picture lingo and yelled, "Cut!") Wherever the call came from was academic; the cameras were put back into their cases. It was a wrap.

The scene I started to describe at the opening of this chapter was similar to ones we had filmed many times before, in a number of variations, for many episodes of *Naked City*. Basically, the scene depicts a "heavy" (bad guy) fleeing the police somewhere on the classic rooftops of Manhattan or Brooklyn, or, in this case, the Bronx. The skyline of New York City is featured in most of these shots, as the fleeing suspect is seen running perilously close to the edge of the tarpaper-covered roof and usually jumping from one building to another over deep alleyways. We always tried to make these shots as exciting as possible, showing the streets way below the edge of the roof, or shooting up as the suspect ran on the lip of the roof and vaulted the space between buildings. He would be chased in most cases by the police, uniformed actors and stunt performers who in many cases were exchanging gunfire with the fleeing suspect.

That was going to be the case on this chilly fall morning in the Bronx. I was one of three camera operators filming this particular shot from different vantage points. The use of multiple cameras is always in order when something perilous or dangerous is being filmed; we try to cover all the angles at once so the dangerous stunt does not have to be repeated. In this case, I was across the street from a typical, five-story walk-up apartment building, expecting to film the suspect running on the edge of the roof as he is chased by three uniformed cops who are yelling at him to stop. At one point, the action called for the suspect to turn around and shoot at the policemen. The cops hit the deck, take cover behind chimneys, get into the appropriate shooting stance and return fire. Even as we were rehearsing this shot, preparations were going on for the next shots in the sequence: the suspect jumping from one rooftop to the other. On a television series, even complicated and dangerous shots such as these are filmed unceremoniously, routinely and quickly. We would set up, rehearse, shoot and move onto the next setup — a routine that, after a couple of years of shooting the same show, developed into second nature and at times came close to being boring.

That's how I felt that morning. Still somewhat sleepy, I looked at the rehearsals through the camera's viewfinder, made sure that all was ready and waited for the command: "Roll cameras." Of course, there is no gunfire during rehearsal. Even blanks can be dangerous at close range, and although the actors go through the motions and draw their unloaded weapons, instead of firing their weapons, they usually just say, "Bang-bang." The rehearsal went well and all was ready for a take. The actors got into their starting positions and, as usual, according to the routine, my hand reached for the switch, ready to turn the camera on when the "Roll cameras" command came. The cameras rolled, and five stories above the street, the "perpetrator" dashed along the edge of the roof, turning occasionally to fire at the cops in hot pursuit. The cops hit the deck and fired back; the chase was on!

As the camera rolled and I concentrated on the action in the viewfinder, from the corner of my eye I noticed a car coming to a screeching halt in the middle of the street, just a few yards from me. All four doors flew open and four men jumped from the car, leaving it in the middle of the street with doors open. I sensed more than saw the four men running toward the building with our "bad guy" and our "cops" on the roof. Though we were still rolling, my attention left the scene on the rooftop as red warning lights came on and claxons blared in my head, and a gigantic knot quickly formed in my stomach. I saw that all four men had guns in their hands. As usual, I had read the script thoroughly and knew that the four men were not part of our action. Who were they? And why did they stop their car and leave it with its engine running and doors open in the middle of the street? Why were they looking up at the edge of the roof and running full tilt into the building with guns drawn? I thought I knew who they might be. By the time I got into the building, running after them, they were somewhere on the third floor in the narrow staircase of the old tenement. I yelled for them to stop. They did, all four of them leveling their weapons at me. I can tell you I was scared out of my wits at that moment, but my suspicion turned out to be correct: the four men were cops, real cops, with real weapons loaded with real bullets! They were on their way home after the 8 a.m. shift change when they heard gunshots and saw a man running on the roof's edge above them with uniformed cops in pursuit. The man was shooting at the cops, and the cops were returning fire. That was enough to spring the four off-duty cops into action. But fortunately for the actor playing the "heavy," who in a few more seconds could have been lying in a pool of blood on the roof of a Bronx tenement at the end of what could have been a promising acting career, they stopped when I yelled at them and explained we were filming a television show. I was pretty shaken for the rest of the day and shudder now as I write this, trying to come to terms with what could have happened as our highly motivated civil servants sprang into action.

The weekly *Naked City* episodes usually signed off with the booming, resonant voice of the announcer: "There are eight million stories in the naked city. This has been one of them." Indeed it was!

Civil servants, upright citizens driven by a sense of civil responsibility, can and on occasion do step up to the plate when they see something that doesn't seem to be right, something that calls for action as it unfolds before their eyes. In one of Francis Coppola's early movies, *You're a Big Boy Now,* the action of an important sequence called for our hero, Peter Kastner, to run through a busy department store at the busiest time of day carrying a priceless Gutenberg Bible stolen from the New York Public Library. He is chased by a huge, Irish sheepdog with a wooden leg attached to its collar, a uniformed cop (Dolph Sweet), his landlady (Julie Harris), his friend (Tony Bill), his girlfriends (Elizabeth Hartman and Karen Black), his father (Rip Torn) and his mother (Geraldine Page, who received an Academy Award nomination for her work in the movie). No one in the store knew that this scene was going to be filmed, which was not exactly according to the proper practices of the film industry or filmmaking in general, but in this case it was, for a number of reasons, the only way we could film the scene and get the utmost chaos and excitement we hoped to get for the shots. Obviously, we knew we could only do this once, because after the crowds in the store found out that this was part of a movie, they would not react the same way to the same action the second time around. Our cameras were hidden, and the cast rehearsed by walking slowly through the action, following a predetermined route between the aisles of merchandise — of course, without the sheepdog and the screaming cop. This gave the hidden cameras a chance to frame up, focus and compose the shots. No one in the store, other than a few store executives who were in on this bit of unorthodox filming technique, suspected anything.

When the cameras rolled and the action began, pandemonium broke out as some of the "customers" (stunt people) were knocked around and merchandise was sent flying by the actors and the sheepdog with the wooden leg attached to its leash. People where aghast, surprised and scared and desperately tried to get out of the way, except for one young fellow, a model citizen who leaped from one escalator to the other and, with one well-placed punch, knocked our hero, Peter Kastner, out cold. We thought this was a wrap, but in fact, unrehearsed as it was, it became the most valuable part of the scene. When Francis saw the dailies, he re-wrote the scene to incorporate this unrehearsed and unexpected bit of action, and we filmed additional scenes in the studio to round out the sequence. The young fellow who KO'd Peter Kastner became a hero in the store. He was a celebrity for the next half-hour or so and, I imagine, when he and his buddies went to see him in the movie. Peter Kastner nursed a swollen cheek and a couple of black eyes for a while. But this incident, like the *Naked City* incident, turned out all right in the end, though both could have had more serious, perhaps devastating conclusions.

But surprises — the unforeseen, the unexpected and the unrehearsed — lurk around every turn of the road of making movies. Two such things happened on another film, *The Out of Towners* (1970), which stars Jack Lemmon and Sandy Dennis. The picture, a super movie, one of Neil Simon's best, is one laugh after the other. For the benefit of those who may not have seen it or need a reminder, the film deals with a day and a night in the lives of an Ohio couple who come to New York to accept and celebrate a large promotion for the husband and look forward to a great day in the Big Apple. But getting to New York turns out not to be half the fun. Instead of New York, the couple lands in Boston. They get to New York by train, hungry, and find that the city is crippled with all sorts of strikes and their hotel room has been given to someone else. In addition to a transportation strike (no cabs, no buses, no subways) and a shortage of hotel rooms, the couple must contend with a huge storm of tropical proportions, a milk-delivery strike and a garbage strike. As Sandy Dennis puts it in the film, "There is no milk for babies and little children." A garbage strike meant mountains of garbage all over every street as far as the eye could see. And that is exactly how our prop master interpreted Neil Simon's script.

"Props," items in a film that performers use or come in contact with while playing a part, or anything that decorates a set, items that most people in the audience take for granted or may not even notice, can take on a dimension of extreme importance in a Neil Simon movie. Garbage in the shots, the result of a garbage strike, was a "prop," and we had tons of it — tons of garbage that was carefully prepared not to rot, smell or ooze, to be no more disgusting than it had to be for pictorial purposes. This garbage had to be

Jack Lemmon and me in a light moment between takes.

readily handled, stored, transported and stacked to accommodate the requirements of the script and the camera.

Years before *The Out of Towners*, as I was starting out in the film business, an elderly prop man paternally took me into his confidence and explained to me that there were only two kinds of props: "ordinary props," like a telephone on a desk in an office, for example, and what he called significant props. The way this old timer put it — and it made sense to me — ordinary props just appear in the set, but if they weren't all there, the film would not suffer greatly. Without "significant props," on the other hand, the story could not be effectively told, and the film could not be made. On *The Out of Towners*, tons of garbage was "significant" with a capital "S."

The old prop man's words came back to me as I stood one cold April night in front of Grand Central Station in New York, ready to film a portion of the rainstorm scene in which Jack Lemmon and Sandy Dennis get soaked to the skin. Making rain of the magnitude of a tropical downpour is an awesome undertaking, yet as I stood there trying to visualize the scene, what struck me was that in whatever direction I looked, all I could see were mountains and mountains of garbage lining the edge of the sidewalks. I complimented our prop master, who told me that by then he and his crew

Jack Lemmon and Sandy Dennis running in a rainstorm by piles of garbage.

had been working for weeks, stuffing garbage bags (double- and triple-strength so they wouldn't break) and collecting and cleaning residue from hundreds of food containers and cans collected from actual garbage, which they then carefully arranged next to purposely torn garbage bags to make it look like spilled garbage. To these, fresh lettuce leaves, bread wrappers, banana peels, paper bags, newspaper pages and so on were added, all in the name of realism and for the sake of art. And realistic it was. So realistic, in fact, that passersby would occasionally flip an empty cigarette pack at one of the mounds and, in some instances, residents of the area added their own "real" garbage, which, when it went unnoticed, created problems days later as it started to smell. Finding rotting, real garbage amongst the hundreds of bags filled with newsprint, empty boxes and other clean stuffing was not easy. And it took huge trucks to deliver our "garbage" to our locations every day, and to haul it away to storage until it was needed again at our next location.

Because the strikes in the movie continue pretty much throughout the film, after a while, working around the huge mounds of garbage became second nature for cast and crew. We became blasé about it; we knew it would be on the street as we got to work and weren't surprised that it was. Not much thought was given to the garbage beyond that. And so it was that on one beautiful, spring morning....

Well, let me tell you a bit more about the story before I continue talking about garbage, and cut back to another very interesting thing that happened while filming this movie. Our hero couple, Mr. and Mrs. Kellerman (Lemmon and Dennis), now hungry and soaked to the skin, walk out of Central Park, where they spent the night trying to get some sleep but were mugged instead. They are desperate, disheveled, dirty, hungry and penniless in the middle of New York, somewhere on Central Park West. Jack is venting his anger in the middle of the road when his wife hears a hissing sound. She yells to her husband to step back off a manhole cover, which, just as he does step back, blows up with a deafening explosion followed by a column of smoke and dust, shooting the 4-foot-diameter manhole cover high up into the air like a missile. Of course, this was not an unexpected, accidental thing. The script called for it, and the special effect was carefully designed and constructed to blow the manhole cover high into the air and, according to the script, drop it in slow motion onto a brand-new convertible Cadillac, obliterating the car. The entire sequence was carefully described in the script, which contained all the various shots of the sequence.

But the sequence didn't turn out quite the way it was depicted in the script. All went according to plan up to the point when Sandy yelled at Jack to step back as the massive manhole cover was blown into the air. From there on, the action stopped following the script. The massive manhole cover, an exact replica of the real thing reproduced in lightweight balsa wood, flew up three or four stories high like a rocket and was calculated to land some distance from Jack, out of the shot. The cast-iron real thing could not have been blown into the air and would have been extremely dangerous

A moment between takes: Neil Simon, me and director Arthur Hiller.

if it had been. But the replica was also large, about 4 inches thick, and was heavy enough to be handled by two special-effects men. Jack's reaction was the best piece of acting I have ever seen. As the ferocity of the explosion knocked him back, his expression was at the same time surprised and frightened. He knew that the shot called for the explosion and his reaction to the explosion. That was to be the end of the shot, but as professional as Jack Lemmon was, he was going to go on acting until the director called "Cut." But the director, Arthur Hiller, probably enjoying Jack's performance, didn't call "Cut." The cameras continued to run and Jack continued to act, even as the manhole cover came crashing down — not on the Cadillac, but just inches in front of Jack's face, nearly decapitating him. But the trooper in Jack surfaced. He continued to stagger around, acting his part to the hilt, never reacting to what could have been a devastating, possibly fatal situation. He went on turning in a fantastic, unrehearsed performance, which is what ended up in the movie. The Cadillac was spared, and fortunately, Jack didn't have as much as a scratch on him. We ended up with a priceless bonus shot that no planning or rehearsals could have given us.

The Out of Towners, like so many other films, had its share of these sorts of unforeseeable incidents. One not as potentially dangerous as the incident I described above still brings a smile to my face, though it caused a huge problem when it happened. I already mentioned that as part of the film's story, New York City was plagued by strikes, one of which was a garbage strike. All garbage collection was at a standstill in the city, and wherever the camera

A moment before "Action." Sandy Dennis and Jack Lemmon prepare to enter a low-angle shot as Arthur Hiller and I stand by.

looked, mounds of garbage lined the sidewalks. There was garbage everywhere.

Or perhaps I should say there was no garbage anywhere. As you recall, early in this chapter I explained that our prop department took large truckloads of carefully created "prop" garbage with us everywhere we went and put the garbage out in huge mounds wherever the camera pointed. This "garbage" was prominently featured in the film and had to look perfect down to the last torn and spilled bag, including such small touches as empty milk cartons, lettuce leaves, melon rinds, old shoes, newspapers and so on. After each shot was "in the can," the garbage was carefully collected and loaded into the trucks or laid out for the next shot as needed. One of the biggest of these shots was scheduled for one morning near the spot where the manhole cover blew up. The camera was going to see a very large area of the west side of Manhattan, and extra garbage had to be created and brought to the location to dress up several city blocks. It took the entire morning just to construct the mounds of garbage for the action of the scene in a way that looked best to the camera. Then, when all was set and in place, it was time for the company to break for lunch.

When the lunch hour was over and the crew was trickling back to the corner of Central Park West and 64th Street, a most astonishing sight greeted us. A quiet voice that embodied our worst fear summed it up best: "Where is the garbage?" There wasn't an ounce of garbage anywhere in sight. All of the garbage that had taken the entire morning to carefully arrange for the camera's best advantage was gone. It had disappeared without a trace, without as much as a single sheet of torn newspaper left on the street. We were shot down. We couldn't shoot without our "significant prop," the garbage. An hour or so later, the rumors started circulating about some irate citizen calling City Hall with a complaint about mountains of uncollected garbage. His complaint was so effective that within a short time, a convoy of garbage trucks arrived and picked up our carefully constructed, artfully arranged "garbage." It wasn't long before an announcement came from a bullhorn, just as a city garbage truck disappeared around a corner way down the street: "Check your call sheets for the time of call tomorrow. It's a wrap!"

In retrospect, all these incidents bring on a smile now and are high on the list of fond memories. The real cops didn't shoot our actor, Jack Lemmon wasn't hurt, and the garbage was replaced. We were not that lucky on another film, where the star of the project, the beloved actor Bert Lahr, died during the filming.

THE COWARDLY LION

Children and adults the world over grieved when they heard that the much-loved character from the movie *The Wizard of Oz,* the Cowardly Lion, Bert Lahr, had passed away. Bert was and will be remembered by generations to come as the Cowardly Lion, who would dance around those he wanted to intimidate, raising his fists in the manner of a prizefighter, saying, "Huff, huff, put 'em up, put 'em uuup!" In the end, Bert Lahr did put them up. He waged a spectacular fight to the end, dying in the middle of the filming of a star-studded movie, *The Night They Raided Minsky's.*

It was early spring when I received a call from Norman Lear, whom I had heard of but never met. He and his partner, Bud Yorkin, were well known for their very successful television shows, which is why I was surprised to hear that he wanted to talk to me about shooting a feature film. He suggested that I join him and his director, Billy Friedkin, for lunch to get acquainted and see if we might be right to work with one another. Though I had done two very successful and highly recognized films by that time, *One Potato, Two Potato* and Francis Coppola's *You're a Big Boy Now,* any feature film held out hope for a continued and successful career in movies. Needless to say, I was delighted. This movie, *The Night They Raided Minsky's,* was going to be a big-budget musical produced by Norman Lear for United Artists. Academy Award winner Arnold Schulman wrote the script, and the cast was to include Jason Robards Jr., Britt Ekland, Norman Wisdom, Forrest Tucker, Joseph Wiseman, Bert Lahr, Elliot Gould, Harry Andrews, Denholm Elliott, Jack Burns and quite a few other notables. Before going to our lunch meeting, I asked around about William Friedkin, whom I had not heard of, and was pleased to learn that he was widely regarded as the new "boy genius" of the industry. I also read the script, which Norman sent to my home on Long Island by messenger on the day of our conversation, and found out that the movie was a period piece, taking place in the mid-1920s. It was going to be about the birth of burlesque in New York and, interestingly, it was supposed to have been based on a true story.

The lunch turned out to be very pleasant. Norman Lear was a straightforward, down-to-earth sort of guy, and Billy Friedkin, just as his reputation suggested, seemed to be talented, interested, very pleasant and very much committed to the project. He had done a great deal of research by that time and knew a lot about the history of burlesque in New York, and his ideas about how to approach and execute the film seemed right — in fact, very interesting — to me. He told me he was assembling a great circle of talent for the film. He had already tied up John Lloyd, the well-known production designer, and the highly regarded husband-and-wife team of art directors, Bill and Jean Eckar; and he was talking with, he told me, the equally well-known choreographer Danny Daniels. I knew some of the people and had heard of most of the others, and as I listened to Billy I tried very hard to conceal how pleased I was to be even considered to possibly be part of this distinguished group. By the time we got through dessert, it seemed like my doing the film was a done deal, that I had landed the biggest plum yet at that point in my career. I was near seventh heaven as we shook hands after lunch.

I re-read the script as soon as I got home and started making notes to be better prepared the next time Billy or Norman called. But much to my dismay, no call came. As the days went by, I began to hear rumors, which turned out to be true, that, in fact, Billy Friedkin was contacting just about all the New York cinematographers, including some who were older and much better known than I, with much broader backgrounds than mine and many great credits to their names. I even learned that one of these

Top: Rehearsal. Bottom, left to right: actors Harry Andrews, Bert Lahr, Forrest Tucker and Dick Libertini and me.

cinematographers, Ernie Caparros, a well-known television-commercial cinematographer with whom I worked often as a camera operator, had already visited many of the film's locations with Billy. This was generally interpreted in the industry as a step past being tied to the project. Because this man was a friend, I decided to call him. He confirmed my fears, as he told me that he was going to be the director of photography of *The Night They Raided Minsky's*. Though I was very disappointed — it's never easy to lose a promising project — this was just another incident where I lost out to a better-known person. "Oh, well!" I probably said, put the script away and went on with my life.

Six, maybe seven weeks later, by which time I had gotten over the loss of *Minsky's*, I was shooting a television commercial on the train tracks way out from the Los Angeles railroad station when a production assistant handed me a note to call a Mr. Friedkin as soon as possible. In the pre-cellphone days, when one was shooting on location, returning a phone call generally meant waiting for the next break in the work — lunchtime, for instance — and at times the entire break would be used up returning and making telephone calls. I was told that Mr. Friedkin was waiting for my call and was put right through to him. He could not have been friendlier. When he found out that I was shooting a commercial, he told me commercials were the best proving ground for film people and said he also liked working on them. He wanted to know if I was going to be ready to start *Minsky's* by a certain date. I told him I had heard that he'd decided to go with my friend, but he explained that I was locked in at our first lunch; he just wanted to make sure that he investigated all possibilities and was making the right choice. There was never any doubt in his mind, he insisted, that I was the right person for the movie. Needless to say, I didn't argue the point, but I wondered what would have happened if, in the interim, I had accepted another film. When Billy and I finished talking, Norman Lear came on the phone and wanted to know if I was still interested in the project. I assured him that I was, and he promised to send my contract to the Beverly Hills Hotel, where I was staying while doing commercials in Los Angeles.

I still had no agent — not that I didn't want one, but none of the better agents was interested in talking with me. Most young people just starting out in the movie business are convinced that if they can get an agent, their future, fame and fortune will be instantly ensured. Nothing could be further from the truth. Agents, I learned, are not interested in representing anyone unless the person is in demand and, as they say, an "easy sell." Simply put, agents won't jeopardize a higher fee for themselves by trying to promote a person who is not in demand and risk losing a project that could have gone to one of their better-known clients. On the other hand, when a person is in demand, recognized and sought after by the industry, agents come knocking on the door. That is exactly what happened to me after I accepted and started shooting *Minsky's*. The top agent in Hollywood at that time, Mortie Gutterman, called me — I couldn't get past his secretary till then — and wanted to know if I was represented and, if not, would I want to discuss representation with him. He offered to come to New York to meet me, which he did, and

Professor Spats (Bert Lahr) in bowler hat. Director Billy Friedkin (wearing glasses) is at Bert's right. I'm the fellow wearing the necktie, behind the bullhorn.

we started a client/agent relationship that grew into a great friend-ship and lasted 14 years. Had he been representing me when the contract was delivered to me at the Beverly Hills Hotel, he would have, I've no doubt, made a much better deal for me than I did. But I wasn't unhappy with my deal and was looking forward to doing *The Night They Raided Minsky's*.

As soon as I got back to New York, I went to see Billy and Norman. I started prepping the film almost immediately, re-read-ing the script, making notes of things I wanted to research and discuss with Billy and others, and, above all, getting a crew together. *Minsky's* was going to be a big production, far bigger than anything I'd done till then. Billy and I had countless meet-ings, at times over lunch in some of the most famous restaurants in New York, The 21 Club, The Russian Tea Room and so on. We also frequently met early in the morning or late at night, when-ever our busy schedules allowed it, or immediately when the situ-ation demanded it. I visited libraries and museums, researching material that dealt with the era of the movie, and pored over material collected by the Eckars and Billy. There were endless discussions about the film's look, specifically how I was going to portray the period in color when everybody who remembered that era remembered it as they saw it in newsreels: in black-and-white. The film had to be photographed in color. Black-and-white movies were hard to sell and distribute by that time and were not popular with the public or with theater owners. The script called for the film to start with old newsreel footage. We decided to inte-grate this old footage with our own, which was to be photographed in color but printed in black-and-white, then scratched and beat up to match the old newsreel footage that was to open the movie. At a certain point during the opening of the film, the "scratches" and "tears" of our "old" footage would disap-pear and the image would slowly turn into brilliant color. In the end, this technique worked extremely well, transferring an old, black-and-white era into color for the rest of the movie. Attesting to its success, the technique was much imitated on other films.

We prepared the film for many weeks. Several city blocks

were magically returned to the bygone era of the Twenties. These blocks, on the east side of Manhattan, were scheduled to be demolished, and the city government turned them over to us, giving us a gigantic back-lot set. The buildings were repainted to look like they did in the Twenties; broken windows were replaced; and signs, some in Hebrew, Russian and in the lettering of other languages, were painted to look either new or beat up, just as they looked in the old photographs we collected about that era. On the days of shooting, these streets were teeming with people in period clothes, and pushcarts and horse-drawn wagons were everywhere. Our company also took over an old theater on Second Avenue that was still used occasionally for XXX-rated films only. We restored the marquee and the interior of the theater to near their original splendor.

It was a magical moment to suddenly find myself in the mid-1920s on the first day of the shooting, preparing to film the first shot of our schedule in front of this theater. The first shot, I remember as clearly as if it were yesterday, was a close-up dolly shot of a pair of feet energetically walking on the sidewalk. Besides striped, gray period slacks and high, lace-up shoes, the actor also wore spats, an item of clothing not seen today that was made from cloth with many buttons and worn over one's shoes. The character wearing these spats was called "Spats" or "Professor Spats," and was played by Bert Lahr. Billy introduced me to Mr. Lahr just minutes before we made the shot, and I still recall how hard it was for me to suppress my excitement as I shook hands with the Cowardly Lion. Bert Lahr was best known at that time (and perhaps for all time) as Zeke, the friendly, smiling, young fellow who worked on the Kansas farm where Dorothy lived in *The Wizard of Oz*. In the ensuing months, while filming *Minsky's*, I got to know Bert Lahr well. I was awed by his presence and pleasant personality and spent every minute with him that I could afford during a very intense production.

Although we put in long, hard days of work, every day on the job was filled with fun and excitement for me. The sets, particularly the interior of the theater and the location exteriors, were magnificent. Walking the streets amongst costumed extras reminded me of all the old, faded, sepia-tone photographs I researched. None of the kids in period clothes playing games on the street between takes or the other extras paid any attention to me, which made me feel as if I were invisible, thrown back into history by some kind of time machine. Even the smells on these streets — freshly baked breads, all kinds of other foods, middle-European smoked meats, fresh fish on ice, horses and even horse droppings — made these sets magically transport me back to a bygone era.

News of the filming spread, and within a short time we had a very large problem keeping tourists who flocked to our outdoor sets out of the pictures. Time and again while watching dailies, we would discover a person in contemporary dress with a camera amongst our period-clad extras, and the shot would have to be retaken. The tourists flocking to see our set became a big problem, and eventually the set had to be closed to all but cast and the crew. Likewise, extreme care had to be exercised not to photo-graph anything that would suggest a later era. Television antennas had to be removed from rooftops that were going to be seen in some of the shots, and we had to avoid seeing some of the bigger buildings of New York that surrounded our set but were built later than the Twenties. On the other hand, horse droppings were not picked up; in fact, they were meticulously maintained on the streets, as they were very much part of that era and added an important detail to the film.

Working in the old theater was also extremely enjoyable. The music was great, and the atmosphere of that era was as real as we could have made it for a movie. Every member of the cast and the chorus was hand-picked, including all sorts of Broadway char-acters like Professor Spats. The dancers were picked with the same care. True to the era and the type of theater burlesque was then, more than a few of the dancers were a bit over-age, in some cases overweight and flabby, and in all cases overly made-up. The most interesting aspect about the dancers was that Danny Daniels, one of Broadway's top choreographers, took weeks to teach the girls how to

Director Billy Friedkin checks the camera with me looking on.

dance badly. Perhaps "badly" is not the best way to describe the dancing, but the girls had to perform like those who danced in the burlesque shows of the Twenties, who were neither top performers nor the best dancers, nor the most beautiful. Indeed, our girls, the chorus line of *Minsky's*, was a colorful group. As they danced, they missed a step here and there or slipped and lost their balance now and then, making the numbers fun and very enjoyable to watch.

According to the script, Minsky's burlesque had two performances daily, one in the afternoon and a second in the evening. The afternoon performance was usually for only a handful of drunks who would stagger into the theater to look at the girls and fall asleep. The evening performances were for a somewhat better audience, who came to enjoy the show. When, according to the script, news of Mademoiselle Fifi shedding all her clothes in one of the performances spread through the town like wildfire, the theater filled to capacity night after night with a screaming, applauding audience of New York's high society in evening clothes, all hoping to see the gorgeous Mademoiselle Fifi *au naturel.* The excitement on the days when we filmed in the theater full of people was contagious and soon spread to the crew, and especially to the performers.

Good filmmaking practice dictated that we film each number on the stage from the point of view of the audience, but without an audience. The cameras photographed the performers onstage in wide angles, showing the stage from one side to the other, and then re-shot each number in "coverage," that is to say, focusing on close-ups of the performers' faces, the dancers' feet, and even the orchestra playing vintage instruments in the orchestra pit. When all this coverage was completed, the musical and dance numbers having been photographed, several days were scheduled for the photography of the audience. The afternoon audience was usually photographed in subdued light, making the theater dark and dingy, as bored performers went through their numbers as though they were playing to an empty theater. In contrast, the evening performances, particularly the ones with the audience in evening clothes, were photographed with all the lights blazing, and the atmosphere was electric. On those days, the cameras were set up to shoot angles that incorporated the audience, shooting from behind them at the stage or showing the performances in the foreground of the shots with the audience facing the camera. We scheduled countless shots of the audience as they watched the show, focusing on group shots as well as individual reactions.

I have to digress here for a moment and point out that one filmmaking practice all productions want to avoid is making retakes of scenes that have already been photographed. Retakes, whether they are necessitated by mistakes or by reasons that could not have been foreseen, are costly. The unforeseen factor was the case in *Minsky's,* when we shot the scenes with a theater full of people. Our audience was made up of professional motion-picture extras, people who are not really actors but appear mostly in the background, without specific roles in the story, such as diners in a restaurant, people on the street, soldiers on a battlefield and so on. Their designation, "background extras," adequately states their purpose and function in a film.

In our case, when the "background extras" filled the auditorium to capacity, the lights dimmed, the curtains opened, and suddenly the people in the auditorium, the "background extras," found themselves watching a super production of comedy routines and lavish musical and dance numbers. Though they didn't pay to see this show, and in fact were paid to be the audience, they were enthralled by the performances onstage and reacted accordingly. Their unrehearsed, genuine and enthusiastic reactions filled the auditorium with excitement. The performers on the stage, sensing and being stimulated by this excitement, reacted in turn by delivering livelier performances that were far better and richer than the ones we had filmed the first time, without an audience. Watching our actors being turned on by the audience's obvious enjoyment of their performances, both Billy and I realized that the footage of the same scenes we had photographed some days before was dull, flat and uninteresting by comparison. We also knew that if we wanted to capture the magic of these electrifying performances, we had to act quickly, before the audience's interest waned and before the cast became tired of repeating numbers. I quickly had the camera assistants change lenses on the cameras to get close-up coverage, as the cast was about to perform some numbers for the second time and other numbers the audience had not yet seen. Billy and I both knew that the close-up coverage of our cast responding to the reactions of an enthusiastic audience was important, and the long shots, in which the performers were far from the cameras and small in the frame, could be photographed later. We re-photographed all the numbers, all the coverage, as the audience enjoyed the show — applauding, yelling and whistling — and our cast turned in performances we could not have gotten without the prompting of an audience enjoying the show.

For me, the photography of *Minsky's* was a never-ending, fun-filled process of creating colorful images and enjoying brilliant performances. The tunes and music of the old Broadway stage and the jazz of smoke-filled nightclubs of that era still ring in my ears. The experience of working on this movie, as many crewmembers commented frequently, was too good to believe. And there were other benefits also.

One of our main sets was a typical, Broadway-style, Jewish delicatessen. Though the set was built on the sound stage, it looked and smelled real because all of the foodstuffs — supplied by the Hebrew National Food Company — were real. We had smoked meats of all kinds, corned beef, pastrami, smoked tongue, sausages and salami by the ton. Whereas on most other films these foodstuffs would be kept until the filming was completed, Hebrew National insisted that all food would have to be fresh, and that their own people would appear in the film as the staff behind the counter. The deli was restocked with fresh food every day before filming started, and every evening, the crew, myself included, went home with bags full of wonderful deli products. For weeks, as the filming was going on in the deli set, my family and I enjoyed wonderful all-beef, kosher hot dogs, sour pickles and hard salami on fresh-baked rye bread.

The film was coming together beautifully. We would gather on some weekends in a projection room to see cut sequences, and even though they were in a rough stage, all of us were convinced that we had an unusual, terrific film on our hands that was going to be very successful when it was released. Then tragedy struck.

We were about two-thirds of the way through the filming when we arrived on location one late afternoon for night work. It was a dreary, drizzly fall evening. I didn't like the cold but didn't

While I watch from behind the camera, director Billy Friedkin rehearses with actors Jason Robards and Forrest Tucker.

mind the drizzle, as it gave the pavement a magical quality, reflecting distorted images of the colorful shop windows and the warm glow of yellowish street lamps. The only thing I recall about this night's work was a take of Professor Spats walking hurriedly, almost jogging, up the street. The camera was to travel with him on dolly tracks, and after a brief rehearsal, we had the first take "in the can." Being a professional as always, Bert Lahr's performance was faultless — at least, I thought so. But for some reason, Billy didn't. We made several more takes, but the slight upgrade of the street made running difficult, and after each take Bert appeared to be more and more tired, almost completely spent. After some additional takes, Billy accepted Bert's performance. Though not in bad shape, Bert was 72 years old and not very athletic. As a pro, he would have run the street as many times as Billy insisted on or until he dropped, but when wrap was called, it was obvious to all that Bert would not have been able to make many more takes. He was perspiring heavily and looked visibly wrung out as he sat quietly in his chair. Three or so days later, we heard that Bert came down with a cold, had a high fever and could not work for a while. The shooting schedule had to be readjusted, as they say in the business, "to shoot around him." By that time in the schedule, this was not easy. Bert was in almost all the scenes we still had to film. He understood the situation and came back to work in about a week, claiming to be much better, but all of us knew, or sensed, that this was not the case. He didn't look well. His face was haggard and he seemed to have lost a lot of weight. The wardrobe department confirmed the weight loss when it was found that every piece of Bert's wardrobe was too big for him. The costumes were re-tailored to fit him, and we went ahead with filming his scenes. But the old pizzazz, his energy and his professionalism, were not the same. He seemed to be tired all the time, his smile was forced, and it was not difficult to see how hard he had to work at forcing himself to play his part. Every move, even getting out of a chair, pained him, and the pain was obvious.

The company fixed up one of the old dressing rooms behind the stage for him with comfortable armchairs and a sofa, and between takes Bert would retire to this room with his wife to rest. I spent as much time as I could with him and listened to his stories about his life in show business. I didn't want to tire him, but he seemed anxious to talk. He told me about his childhood in New York, dropping out of school, and his early days in the theater and vaudeville and eventually in burlesque. He was the one member of our group, cast and crew, who was actually part

Director Billy Friedkin, producer Norman Lear and I, check the script.

of the burlesque scene in the mid-1920s. In fact, he became the unofficial consultant, telling us at times how certain things really happened in the early days of burlesque in New York. I treasured the moments when, in the privacy of his room, I was his only audience. I spent more than a few of my lunch hours with him, but he no longer ate lunch. One day, I still recall, he was telling me fondly about a very successful performance he gave somewhere, and he described it as a "slapper." When he saw the blank look on my face, he explained what a "slapper" was: when a comedian onstage told a good joke well, some in the audience would laugh and slap their legs, and the joke would be classified as a "slapper." Later on, the expression came to denote a great comedy performance. But his performances no longer qualified as "slappers." He was tired and weak, and most of the time he couldn't even remember his lines.

The next bad news came some days later, when we heard that Bert was in the hospital. The rumor mill was at high pitch, speculating about his illness; it was said to be some sort of cancer or pneumonia, but nobody knew for sure and none of us really wanted to speculate. Then I heard that even though he was in the hospital, he was going to continue to work and would come to the stage when he was needed. Amazingly, he did come to work. He would arrive in an ambulance and was brought to the stage in a wheelchair. It was quite shocking to see him. He had lost even more weight, so much, in fact, that his costumes could no longer be re-tailored. His clothes had to be padded to approximate his weight and size in his earlier scenes, but one thing the costume department or any of the other departments could not do anything about was his face. The size and shape of his usually-pudgy face had shrunk dramatically; his eyes were deep-set, his skin was stretched over his skull, and the broad, friendly smile of Zeke/Cowardly Lion, the burly farmhand, was now a grotesque, forced grin filled with pain. On the few occasions when he was brought to work in an ambulance, I went to see him and took him some tea, and for a few minutes I listened to more of his stories, which he still enjoyed and wanted to tell. But by that time, talking caused him so much pain that I would break away and let him rest.

During one of the last of these conversations, I recall him telling me how much he regretted that not too many people recognized him as the actor who had played the Cowardly Lion. What bothered him even more, as he related to me one day, was what happened when a little girl and her mother stopped him as he was strolling on Park Avenue in New York and asked for his autograph. Bert was pleased until he found out that the little girl recognized him not as the Cowardly Lion, but as the "Potato Chips Lady." Bert did a series of very popular television commercials for a potato-chip company dressed as a fat woman in a comical dress. I clearly remember that image, though I can't recall anything else about the commercials. The way he regretfully put it, he spent a lifetime in show business and millions of people all over the world saw him in one of his most memorable performances as the Cowardly Lion in *The Wizard of Oz*, but what he was remembered for was the one-minute-long television commercial in which he appeared as the "Potato Chips Lady." That was the last time I saw Bert. A few days later, it was a wrap for him. He died of cancer in the hospital on December 4, 1967.

Minsky's went on filming after Bert's death, but the high spirit of the production was gone. Some of the scenes featuring Bert that had not been filmed had to be dropped, while others were filmed with look-alikes, mimics and impersonators. It was amazing that well-known impersonators, even some known for their Bert Lahr impersonations, would come up short when their performances as Professor Spats were cut into the film next to a performance by Bert. Caricaturists can enlarge a characteristic feature of a person's face to the extent that the person is instantly recognized by most who see the caricature, but these exaggerations are extreme and are instantly obvious next to a photograph of the person they portray. As I worked with the many impersonators and mimics acting Professor Spats' part in Bert's wardrobe, I found the same was true of them. We photographed the impersonators from behind, using mimics for Bert's voice, but none was good enough to completely or even adequately cover for Bert's absence. As good as some of the performances were, the impersonations were a far cry from the real Bert. A lesser performer, perhaps, could have been successfully impersonated, but not Bert Lahr.

There was a tremendous effort made by the film's editor, Ralph Rosenblum, to save the show. He did a great job using images of Bert photographed earlier in the production, but these cuts would only sustain for seconds or fractions of seconds at a time. Some very creative and clever editing effects and an equally creative soundtrack helped a bit, but without the spark of the real Professor Spats, the film was a wrap.

The Night They Raided Minsky's was released in 1968 and was a modest success, but not what it could have been had Bert been able to finish it. The photography of the movie was mentioned widely and, I'm happy to say, often imitated by television commercials, which was (and still is) one of the highest forms of acknowledgement of good photography by the industry.

Filmmaking, unlike a desk job, poses a danger to personal well being. In the best interest of the movie, filmmakers go out of their way to make a shot or a sequence more interesting, exciting and a bit larger than life. At those times, one takes chances, pushes the limits of safety a bit and at times pays the price. One way or the other, we are all achievers; all of us want to do our respective jobs well, better than anyone, as we compete and try to be the best. An incident that illustrates this is described in the next chapter.

THE FIRST CIVILIZED
MAN ON THE SPOT

Throughout this volume, I allude to the fact that one of the big pluses of spending half a century in cinematography was going to interesting places and meeting interesting people. Ranking high on my list of interesting places, perhaps one of the most interesting, was the then-largely-uncharted interior of Venezuela, where I had a chance to spend a considerable length of time with Lowell Thomas, the great author, explorer and syndicated television newscaster. Mr. Thomas was, without a doubt, one of the most interesting people I ever met and got to know well. The project that took us to Venezuela was a documentary television show, *High Adventure with Lowell Thomas*, which visited and documented some of the most interesting and unusual places and events the world over.

The particular show I was going to film centered on the photography of Angel Falls, the world's highest waterfall, deep in the interior of Venezuela. The falls were named after an American bush pilot, soldier-of-fortune adventurer Jimmy Angel, who, while looking for gold and diamonds, had to make an emergency landing on the plateau above the falls. He somehow walked out of the dense and treacherous jungle to bring news of the immense waterfall. In subsequent years, the falls became better known as more and more people saw them from the air, but we were told that no "civilized" person had ever seen, photographed or measured its true height from the ground up. And that was the objective of our expedition with Mr. Thomas: to go into the interior with a good-sized expedition, locate a spot somewhere around the base of the falls, measure its height and photograph it from the base up.

Needless to say, when the opportunity to be amongst the first civilized people to visit this remote, still-virgin corner of the planet came my way, I jumped at it.

I had been in Venezuela briefly on another film project, but most of that time was spent in Caracas and at the fabulous tourist resorts of Venezuela's north shore. As great as that experience was, the prospect of being a genuine explorer, going to uncharted territory, filled me with anticipation and excitement. Though I was told that this expedition was not going to be easy, nothing could have kept me from participating in it.

The preparations for the project started in New York, where the expedition's organizers and leaders outfitted the crew with proper clothing and equipment and gave us malaria-prevention pills and other shots that were recommended for that part of the world. Unfortunately, the expedition did not have my sizes in clothing, but I was told that my items would be shipped ahead of us to Caracas, and I would be outfitted there.

When the filming in Caracas was completed, my jungle outfit still had not materialized and I was becoming a bit concerned, but in view of the repeated assurances of the expedition leaders that my stuff would be waiting for me at base camp, I boarded the Venezuelan air force DC-3 destined for our jumping-off point, Canaima, in the interior. The flight inside the hot, humid, noisy, smelly and rickety old plane — in spite of the plane bouncing around like a Ping-Pong ball in the hot-air currents over the jungle — strangely enough added to my anticipation of the adventure to come. When the flight was finally over and we landed on the primitive jungle strip, I was rewarded by one of the most beautiful sights I have ever seen. Canaima was situated on the sandy shores of an immense lagoon fed by two huge waterfalls in the distance. The distance tamed the thunderous roar of the falls to a pleasant murmur that lulled one to sleep at night and awakened one gently in the morning. The little community of Canaima consisted of some basic Quonset-type huts and a few thatch-roofed buildings. Aside from some Indians, we were met by Rudi Truffino — "Jungle Rudi," as he liked to be called — a Yugoslavian

Before the first run. Rudi Truffino and me in a boat with the camera on a low tripod. Safety man (with hat) in water. Director Hamilton MacFadden on shore.

emigrant who moved to Venezuela in the late Forties. The only other people at Canaima were a German couple that seemed to be totally out of place in the jungle. They seemed highly educated, and most of us speculated about why such well-educated people should choose to live in such a remote place, away from all the comforts of civilization, without any apparent reason or explanation. Harvey Genkins, my assistant, referred to them as "the Nazis," an assumption I shared, but obviously neither Harvey nor I had proof of our theories. In retrospect, I think we might have been close to the truth.

Our stay in Canaima was delightful. The weather was balmy, breezy and paradise-like. We did a lot of filming in and around Canaima as we prepared for our trip upriver on the Rio Carrao and Rio Churun toward "Salto Angel," Angel Falls. The expedition leaders were hiring Indians, buying huge dugout canoes and outfitting them with outboard motors. Unfortunately, my jungle outfit did not materialize, and I had to make do with some items from my Saks Fifth Avenue wardrobe.

On a number of occasions, Lowell Thomas, my crew and I went off to film some of the scenes for our documentary, at times accompanied by a gentleman, Tom Gilliard, who joined our expedition from the Museum of Natural History in New York. He was an ornithologist who was looking forward to making a collection of insects, moths and other flying creatures such as the vampire bats of the region. At times we traveled by two broken-down Jeeps or on foot, usually staying away from base camp overnight or for a couple of days. One of these trips took us to a section of Auyán-tepuy, a foreboding mountain that is said to have inspired the book *Lost Continent* by Arthur Conan Doyle; it was shrouded in thick, black clouds filled with flashes of lightning most of the time. We traveled light, carrying only the most essential elements of our gear, knowing that our superstitious Indians would only go with us to a certain point, beyond which we would have to carry whatever we brought with us. The mountain was called Devil's Mountain, but instead of hell we were greeted by the sight of a plateau covered with the most beautiful orchids, miles and miles of them as far as the eye could see. We scaled some pretty foreboding cliffs, but the effort was worth it, as the sight and aroma of these flowers were breathtaking. As interesting as the trip was, it didn't turn out to be the mysterious, adventure-laden, *Lost Continent* type of experience I anticipated. The area is a rainforest of lush but gloomy vegetation that is almost continuously enclosed in low clouds. We did some photography and went back to Canaima.

Because Lowell occasionally had to go back to the States, we had to schedule the photography that involved him around his availability. One of the sequences called for him shooting the rapids in a dugout canoe with an Indian up front and another in the rear of the canoe. We were very fortunate to find a great location for filming these shots, Salto Yuri on the Carrao River, not too far down river from Canaima. This spot could not have been better suited to our purposes. All of us thought the photography could be accomplished more easily there than at any of the other nearby rapids. The rapids were similar to the ones we were going

to encounter on our way to Angel Falls — fast, rocky and turbulent — but this section was manageable, as alongside the whitewater section the rapids widened out into a large body of calm
water. The calm section was going to allow us to do tracking shots
alongside the turbulent rapids with the camera in an aluminum
boat powered by an outboard motor. We were going to use the
same aluminum boat, driven by Jungle Rudi, to cover other
angles of Lowell's canoe in the rapids, get follow shots of Lowell
and the Indians from behind, and shoot the rapids ourselves in
front of Lowell's canoe. The first shot on the list — negotiating
the turbulent rapids — was shooting from the front with the
Indian dugout carrying Lowell following us. Side angles of
Lowell's canoe and the follow shots were going to be made once
the shots from the front were in the can. The logic behind this
order of shooting was that the follow shots were going to be done
with a double and scheduled when Mr. Thomas was not going to
be available, in order not to expose him to any more danger than
was absolutely necessary.

The Indians, with Lowell in the middle of the canoe, were
hanging onto rocks at the beginning of the run, waiting for the
aluminum boat with me and the camera mounted in it to enter
the rapids in front of them. This was the Indians' cue to release the
rocks and start following us. The rapids at that point were about a
mile long, perhaps a bit more, and when all the shots, front, side
and rear, were combined in editing, the sequence was going to be
long and exciting. The plan was to terminate each run at the end
of the calm water and tow the dugout back to the start to repeat
the shot as many times as necessary. One can never have enough
footage of such action. One never knows which of the takes will
offer more excitement, and the more interesting footage one has,
the more there is for the editors to work with.

Even before the first take was over, while we were still in
the rapids, I knew we had a problem. My camera was chained into
Rudi's boat on a low tripod, shooting backward as we were
running in front of Lowell's dugout, heading down the rapids.
Rudi, operating the outboard engine, was hunched over, but once

Top: Rudi Truffino and waterfalls at Kaneima.

we were in the turbulent water and the boat pitched up and down, he kept popping up into the shot as I tried to keep the Indian dugout in frame. At the end of the run, all I had were short cuts of when the nose of the aluminum boat pitched up and I was able to shoot over Rudi's head. When we got back to our starting point, we changed the camera over to a tall tripod, which I figured would be high enough to shoot over Rudi and allow me one continuous shot of the entire run.

The Indians were in their starting position once again, holding onto the rocks, waiting for the aluminum boat with the camera to enter the rapids in front of them. Rudi tried to get into the whitewater with the boat facing downstream, but because of the many rocks and the current, we somehow got in front of the Indian canoe at right angles to the current. Something neither I nor anyone else had taken into consideration was that by raising the camera and standing in the boat to look through the viewfinder, I also raised the center of gravity in the boat, making the boat unstable. We turned over almost instantly as the fast current caught us.

Though it seemed like an eternity, the rest of the trip was quick. I was always a good swimmer (good enough to play water polo) and used to being dunked, which helped in this situation, and I finally worked my way out of the rapids into calm water. But I was exhausted and pretty well beaten-up, having been bounced from rock to rock in the foaming, turbulent water for about a mile downriver. The aluminum boat was dented and torn up beyond recognition by the large boulders in the rapids, and Jungle Rudi fared no better than I, but we were alive and, aside from a few minor cuts and bruises, not hurt seriously. The camera and the film, though we recovered them, were a total loss. Days later, when we made the shots again, I mounted the camera into a large Indian dugout that was far better suited for shooting the rapids than the aluminum boat, and when the Indian who was steering the dugout bobbed up into my picture, his presence and image added to the excitement of the shot.

Once all the shots that we could accomplish in the Canaima area were in the can, we were ready to start our trip to Angel Falls. That was the first time I found myself facing off with one of the expedition leaders; let's call him Joe, which, of course, was not his real name. I never hit it off very well with Joe; very few in our group did. He was the one who kept promising my jungle gear, which never materialized, and he was the same fellow who calmly puffed on his pipe, standing onshore, as I was struggling to get out of the rapids. He even had the nerve to tell me how danger-ous the rapids were as I was heading back into the water to help Rudi. I had a few words with him then and never thought much of him afterward. He was supposed to have been a "safety man," an expert outdoorsman and mountaineer, a lifeguard type who was supposed to assist us in dangerous situations.

A notice tacked onto a pole holding up the thatch roof of one of the huts announced that Joe, the expedition expert, was going to lecture that evening after work on the proper method of packing a backpack in preparation for our trip to Angel Falls. All members of the expedition were advised to attend. It is still a

Me and Rudi with the camera on a low tripod in a boat towing the Indian dugout after the first successful run.

mystery to me where or how Joe got hold of a blackboard in the middle of an area that was not even on the map. He must have brought it with him, and I figured that he looked forward to this opportunity to use it. The board had all sorts of charts and diagrams. In front of it, neatly arranged personal items — clothing, canned food, toilet articles and so on — were laid out on a small folding table. Joe's lecture could have bored a first-year Cub Scout to tears, and frankly, I didn't find it any more instructional or interesting. But he droned on, and about an hour or so later, as most everybody was beginning to fidget on the hard benches, I stood up and started to leave. Joe considered himself a self-appointed commanding officer of the expedition and didn't understand the motion-picture hierarchy, so he didn't know that my contract called for photographic services only. He stopped me and told me that unless I stayed and learned how to properly pack my backpack, he would wash his hands and would not help me as I would surely get chaffed, which, he announced with great emphasis, could even turn into "jungle rot." I reminded him that on the basis of his performance, or the lack of it, when I turned

Top: The camera boat with camera on high tripod enters the rapids. Dugout canoe with Lowell Thomas and native follows. Director Hamilton MacFadden is in foreground. Bottom: Dragging the capsized boat out of the water.

Native with blowgun.

over in the rapids, I didn't expect a lot of help from him. Then I explained to him that I really didn't need to know anything about packing a backpack because I'd made a deal with the Indians: they agreed not to take any pictures as long as I promised not to carry anything. With that, I left his lecture, and shortly after I did, most everybody else left also. Ironically, Joe was the only one in our group who was injured while scaling a large rock in the middle of a jungle path. He fell off and sprained his ankle. The rest of us walked around the rock.

The river trip left as scheduled, and we were finally on our way to where no "civilized" person had ever trod. This was true exploration in the virgin territory of the Venezuelan interior, vast areas of which had not been mapped at that time. Rudi knew the river and the area well, as did another European man who joined us, Alejondro (I hope I'm spelling it right) Limey. I am not too sure about his first or last name, but that's how everybody referred to him. For some reason, as the story was explained to me, Alejondro Limey planted and cultivated lime trees around his house in the jungle — South America's answer to Johnny Appleseed, I suppose — and it was suspected that this was behind the name "Limey." He was an interesting and colorful character. I'll be talking more about him and his beautiful, young, blond wife, Yolanda, later in this chapter.

The first day, leaving Canaima, I was probably the only comfortable American member of the expedition in about 15 dugout canoes. I no longer remember how, but I managed to get hold of two surplus G.I.-issue packboards, one of which I rigged into my dugout to sit on, and the other I set up as an adjustable backrest. Those who have ever knelt in a canoe or sat in one without a seat and back support, legs straight in front, for any length of time probably know how most of our people felt by the end of the day when we finally pulled ashore to make camp. By mid-morning the following day, most canoes were similarly rigged, much to Joe's dismay, as backpacks were removed from the packboards and rigged as seats in the dugouts. Most in the group ended up with some sitting arrangements, even those who, as we referred to

Lowell Thomas and native with blowgun at lagoon.

them, went "totally native." No sooner had we landed in Canaima than some of our guys got jungle fever and went "native" by shedding their sneakers and boots, walking around barefoot, letting their beards grow, slitting the legs of their khakis on the side, and making a point of letting everybody see how tough they were as they drank right out of the river. The beards would soon be infested with tiny insects, and the tender soles of city-dwellers' feet would be cut, pierced and bruised by sharp rocks. Other than insect bites, the slit trouser legs did not immediately result in any problems, but drinking the river water drove most of the guys running into the jungle with a roll of toilet paper in hand.

The river trip was truly interesting. Over a number of days, the river that was calm and very wide as we left Canaima narrowed, and the current became fast and angry, in some cases downright unfriendly. All in all, we spent 10 days going upriver and encountered close to 70 rapids, some of which had to be portaged around. We spent some nights high up on the cliffs of narrow canyons for fear of a rainstorm upriver, which, Rudi told us, occasionally sent a 20-foot-high tidal wave down the canyon. We saw high watermarks on the canyon walls and searched for a suitable spot to bed down above those marks. The canoes were tied up with long ropes whenever we could not bring them ashore so that in case of a tidal wave, a short rope would not capsize them or pull them under.

At the end of the tenth day, we arrived at a spot where the river was no longer navigable, and Limey suggested we make our base camp there. The plan was for Limey to set out on foot with some of the Indians and look for a legendary rock from which, the Indians claimed, the entire falls were visible. Limey had never seen this rock, but he had no reason to doubt the Indians. With his rusty, old shotgun and a huge machete in hand, Limey took off to locate the rock. He was a very intriguing fellow. No one ever got very close to him, but the stories Rudi told about him were interesting, to say the least. Limey was a Lithuanian emigrant who, after World War II, ended up in Venezuela. It was interesting to speculate about all these German-speaking Europeans from countries such as Lithuania and Yugoslavia, very likely all Nazis who were possibly hiding in this remote, inaccessible portion of the jungle. Like so many others, Limey was said to have come to the jungle to look for gold and diamonds, and according to Rudi, he was one of a few who actually found diamonds. But the partner who started out with Limey, another Lithuanian, was never seen or heard from again. With a small fortune in diamonds, Limey left the jungle and married Yolanda. As I mentioned earlier, Yolanda was a beautiful, young, Austrian woman. Rudi claimed she was a countess who, for some reason, also left Europe after the war, and when the money ran out, she came back to the jungle with Limey to look for more diamonds. But Yolanda, as I got the story, didn't like the jungle. To her, life in the wilderness didn't tally with Limey's glowing description of it. I got to hear about that because the cigarettes I smoked at the time, Kents, new on the market and advertised as having the latest "Micronite" filter, were her favorites. I came well supplied with Kents, and she much preferred them to the coarse, hand-rolled, jungle variety. She told me that she came to the jungle because Limey's description of the carefree life there sounded like the Garden of Eden, and because Limey told her that he knew of many locations where diamonds and emeralds were sure to be found. She expected her stay in the jungle to be brief. I understood her desire to leave it when I saw the "house," more like a rickety shack, that Limey built for himself and loved, which must have sounded nicer in Limey's description than living in it alongside lizards, scorpions and giant spiders, not to mention other, larger inhabitants of the "jungle paradise." Yolanda was a very pleasant and intelligent young woman with an obviously good middle-European background and education. She spoke several languages, including some Hungarian, which allowed us a certain privacy in communicating. I was sorely tempted when she hinted that I help her leave the jungle, but several things kept me from doing this. One, I was happily married, and two, I didn't want to get mixed up in her domestic life and problems, particularly when I thought of Limey's rusty, old shotgun and oversized machete. Rudi's stories about Limey's partner were good deterrents also. Whenever Yolanda was with Limey, the two of them seemed very much in love, and at those times she didn't seem to mind jungle life. Had I thought that she was in danger in the jungle with Limey, I probably would have tried to help her, but this didn't seem to be the case.

About three days after he left, Limey returned with the Indians and told us that the Indian lore was true: he did find the rock from which the falls could be seen from its top rim to the bottom of the canyon. We set out the following morning on the trail Limey marked, and this time even I carried my share of the load. To say that the going was hard would be an understatement. Sections of the jungle floor were decomposed matter, which over a millennium had built up to form the soil. It was spongy and constantly moved underfoot, undulating like a suspended hammock. At times the smelly surface would cave in unexpectedly and one's leg would suddenly be swallowed up to one's groin. Unexpectedly falling into these holes was frightening as well as painful, particularly with the heavy backpacks we were carrying. Getting out of the holes — even with help — usually turned into a comic performance. We would extricate one leg as the other would sink into the soft, spongy, powdery ground. The trip that took Limey a day took us three days. But Limey was almost like an Indian. He walked, moved and generally behaved like one. He hardly ever talked, and when we had to have a conversation pertaining to some expedition matter, he would always take long pauses before answering, and his ever-present smile, more like a grin, would never fade. He was a good man to have around on the expedition — and, most likely, to stay clear of under other circumstances.

In the late afternoon on the third day, Limey told us that the rock was just ahead and it would be a little climb to get to it. By that time, the majestic, huge horseshoe of the falls was in sight way above and to the right of us, with what seemed like a trickle of water coming over the rim of the horseshoe. During the rainy season, Limey told us, water would be coming over the lip of the entire horseshoe, and the canyon we'd just come through would most likely be entirely under water. At this time of the year, in the middle of the dry season, what looked like one small stream was nevertheless a huge amount of water. The stream, arcing over the lip of the falls, slowly turned to mist as it got closer to the bottom, and the mist was filled with hundreds of dancing rainbows. None of us had any idea how high the falls really were. No one knew, and the estimates ranged from 2,500 to 5,000 feet.

The late-afternoon sun was rapidly creeping up the canyon wall as we spotted the huge rock some distance ahead. The climb didn't appear to be difficult; in fact, there seemed to be a trail leading up to the rock. The excitement of being first at this spot sparked a sort of rivalry and our pace quickened, everybody wanting to get to the rock first. It so happened that I ended up being the "first civilized man" to reach the rock, one of the then-uncharted spots in that virgin wilderness of our planet. One qualification must be mentioned: I was first except for Limey, of course, who reached the rock four days before we did. But to my way of think-

Me with camera at Angel Falls.

ing, and because of Rudi's stories of him, Limey did not fully qual-
ify as "civilized" (no disrespect intended).

There was one other disturbing factor that cast a haze
over my achievement. As I was approaching the rock, slightly out
of breath and still some distance from it, an odd, little, yellow
spot caught my eye near the base of the huge boulder. I didn't
think much of it at first; it could have been a yellow flower or a

yellow rock, though I thought it was curious that it was the only yellow color anywhere in sight. As I got closer, the odd, little, yellow spot took on the shape of a small cube, and even before I got close enough to pick it up I recognized the well-known shape and markings of an Eastman Kodak 35mm Plus-X film box. Finding that box in this spot was, to say the least, devastating. Limey, as far as I knew, did not own a camera. I knew that none of the Indians did. Where did the box come from? Was there another "civilized" man at the spot before me, and was I therefore not the first "civilized" man on the spot? Someone, perhaps Tom Gilliard (I no longer remember), reasoned that somebody photographing the falls from a small plane must have thrown the box out. This made me feel much better, but the doubt, even after all these years, still lingers.

The following day, we photographed the falls from many angles. Some of these shots included angles over the shoulder of Lowell Thomas, who had not come with us and at that moment was preparing his evening broadcast in his New York office. The man in the foreground of these shots was a photo double wearing Lowell's shirt and characteristic hat, surrounded by Indians in loincloths with long blowguns, bows and arrows. Lowell's head on close-up was already in the can, having been photographed some time before in Canaima; he was surrounded by the same group of Indians and was looking up and down, as if he were looking at the falls. The height of the falls was also measured and was pronounced to be 3,400 feet. Several years later, a team from the University of Caracas retraced our trail and measured the falls accurately, establishing its height at 3,212 feet.

It was another pretty evening in the jungle. One who has never seen the equatorial sky from a spot that is totally devoid of lights (such as the reflection of nearby city lights) can have no idea how beautiful such a sky can be — an immense, deep-blue/black canapé studded with zillions of brilliant, sparkling stars that seem close enough to touch. The campfire was dying as we listened on short-wave radio to Lowell Thomas' October 5, 1957, broadcast. Almost his entire broadcast was taken up with Russia's successful launching of *Sputnik*, another "first" that was far more important than my being first at the rock. The Russians beat us to space. The news was devastating. We climbed into our sleeping bags, closed the mosquito nets tightly around us, and thought about starting our trip home the following morning. The expedition was a wrap.

Years later, I had a chance to photograph another documentary that I thought was going to be far less dangerous, far from any jungle or the Arctic, in New York City. It was to be about an invasion of Beatles, and ....

THE YEAR OF THE BEATLES

If the Chinese calendar had been created in the twentieth century, the year 1965 would have surely become known as "The Year of The Beatles." Their reputation preceded them, and by the time they came to New York for the first time, the airport was mobbed by screaming, teenaged girls and other admirers. The Ed Sullivan Theatre on Broadway was likewise mobbed for the Sunday afternoon rehearsal and the Sunday evening show. As I'd heard, the CBS ticket office received more than 70,000 ticket requests for a theater that had the seating capacity of about 700. The police had to be called to control the mob. It is estimated that more than 80 million people watched the show, which firmly established The Beatles in America and did no harm to the popularity of *The Ed Sullivan Show*, either. The practice on the Sullivan show, as I understand it, was that each new act was contracted for multiple performances on the show at a set fee. If the performers, as they say on Broadway, "laid an egg," they would be dropped from the next show's line-up, but if the performance was popular, the option would be exercised for additional appearances. When The Beatles made their first appearance on *The Ed Sullivan Show*, the ratings were the highest of any show on television until then.

I was not a Beatles fan. Perhaps I was too much of an "establishment" type, but with four young children, I wasn't unaware of The Beatles and wasn't 100-percent sure in 1965 that The Beatles were a good influence. I like their music now, years after I filmed them at their first large concert at New York's Shea Stadium, but as one who grew up on Beethoven, Mozart, Chopin, Liszt, Strauss, Lehar and so on, I didn't like their music then, and after filming the concert I swore never to listen to another Beatles number again. The reason for that will be quite obvious. I was not prepared for one aspect of the concert that dramatically affected me. I should have been better prepared, as I should have learned a lesson years before this concert, when …

~ ~ ~

… I got a call from a CBS show, *The Twentieth Century*, to film a sequence for an upcoming episode about the future of air travel. This was in the early Fifties, by which time there was extensive air travel throughout the world, but jet aircraft were still limited to military use only. The show predicted extensive jet travel, and the particular sequence I was to photograph had to simulate a supersonic trip from New York to Washington, D.C. I had to concentrate more on the sensation of the high speed of jet travel than on any other aspect and devise a way to illustrate near-supersonic speeds before there was such a thing for public transportation.

My assistant, Lou Barlia, and I arrived with a small rigging crew at Teterboro Airport in New Jersey, just across the Hudson River from Manhattan, and rigged a rather large camera, a Mitchell NC, onto the bow of an aircraft known as the "Grumman Goose." Dating back to pre-World War II days, this aircraft was considered an antique by that time, but it was the only one I could find that suited my purpose. I had to mount a camera on the outside of the plane, and this aircraft allowed me to do that. The plane was an amphibian, able to operate from water or land. For in-the-water operations, there was a convenient porthole in the bow of the fuselage that a crewmember could crawl to and throw a rope from to somebody on a dock, much the same as if it were a boat. This porthole was just behind where we rigged our camera on top of the fuselage. I was to stand in this porthole throughout the flight to handle the camera, set the exposure and the focus, and point the camera wherever there was something of interest to photograph. I knew that I was going to have to stand half in, half out of the plane and had a good, warm windbreaker with me; the company that supplied the aircraft promised me a helmet, earmuffs to suppress the noise, and goggles. The helmet turned out to be an old, undersized, leather flying gear, similar to ones we see in old photographs of Charles Lindbergh and other early airmen, but they had no earmuffs for me, and the goggles were the type available from five-and-dime stores for kids to use in swimming pools. I shredded my handkerchief and stuffed the small pieces into my ears, managed to get my head into the leather helmet, and, for the lack of a better piece of equipment, put on the swimming goggles. I have to admit that I felt pretty idiotic, and thought I detected suppressed smiles on the faces of my crew and the pilot.

The pilot and I discussed our procedure, signals he wanted me to use to direct him where I wanted to go — up, down, making turns and so on. These were going to be hand signals because radio communication using a microphone would have been useless in the slipstream on the outside of the plane. The pilot warned me not to point backward, because the two propellers of the plane were just a couple of feet behind me. With all of that out of the way, I crawled into the bow and stood in the porthole, my upper torso sticking up out of plane. My rigging crew adjusted my safety harness, a leather belt and some ropes anchoring me into the plane, and we were ready to go. With the use of a piece of equipment called an intervalometer, my camera was adjusted to run at the rate of 1 frame per second instead of the standard 24 frames per second. This meant that it was going to take 24 seconds to produce one second's worth of film, therefore making our flying speed appear to be 24 times faster than it was. I told the pilot to make a much longer than normal ground roll before lifting off at the end of the runway so I could photograph the runway blur under us at a very high speed before the plane leaped into the air. Fortunately, it was a cloudy day, and I signaled the pilot to head for the nearest clouds as soon as it was safe after take-off, knowing that flying close to the clouds would make the plane appear to be flying faster.

I knew I was in trouble the moment the number-one engine fired and the propeller churned up the air behind me with an unbelievable racket. The second engine fired up also, and after a long taxi we got on the runway to take off. The engines revved up, I switched on the camera and we roared down the runway. The slipstream tore the small pieces of my handkerchief from my ears, and the noise of the engines and the props pierced my eardrums, causing excruciating pain. I could not hold my hands over my ears because I had to handle the camera, and I cursed my stupidity for not preparing better for this assignment. Oddly enough, the noise abated some once we were in the air; or, perhaps by that time I was totally deaf. In Washington, I managed to get some cotton for my ears but still had to make do with the goggles. The trip back to Teterboro was not much better, and by the time we landed, all sounds, speech and noise sounded as though they were coming from a great distance, and as though I had a tin bucket over my head. Somehow I managed to tell my assistant to get the film to the lab and drove home with an unbelievable headache, my eyes burning as if someone had thrown sand into them. It was days before my hearing returned and the headache went away completely, and a little longer before I could open and close my bloodshot eyes without pain and eye drops. But the photography of simulated jet travel was interesting, and even standing halfway outside the plane in flight would have been fun if I'd had the right equipment. Within a short time after this experience, I bought a pair of the best earplugs money could buy and a good pair of motorcycle goggles for my kit for future projects. I had a rough experience and looked back on it as a lesson well learned. Or was it?

The Beatles were riding a wave of popularity that was unparalleled by any other group or single performer. By the time they were about to give their first large concert at Shea Stadium in New York, their appearances on *The Ed Sullivan Show* had raised their popularity to an unprecedented level. Feeling the way I did about The Beatles, I wasn't quite certain that I'd done the right thing when I agreed to film this concert. I wasn't and could not have been prepared for the enormity of the project, and could not have even guessed about the difficulties of filming this two-hour-long concert. I found out at the first production meeting that we had no script, but as this project was going to be a documentary, I knew we were going to make up the script as we went along.

PHOTO BY GEORGE E. JOSEPH.

Director Robert Precht and me discussing the filming of the Beatles concert at Shea Stadium.

Clay Adams was going to be the production manager of the project, and Bob Precht was going to be the producer/director. During the early production meetings, Clay, Bob and I tried to figure out how we were going to deal with what lay ahead. We knew from the start that we would have to have multiple cameras to cover all aspects of this unprecedented show, but at that juncture we didn't know how many cameras we were going to need and how they would be deployed and coordinated. I knew that as a documentary, all aspects of the show would have to be filmed, from the early moments of preparation to the last car leaving the vast parking fields around Shea Stadium after the show. But as I worked with schematic diagrams of Shea Stadium, trying to figure out where to place the cameras and what sort of lenses they should have, at every step of the way I discovered that making decisions and determinations about what we were going to do, and how, was easier said than done. I also knew that unforeseen difficulties were all going to add to the problems I was beginning to face.

I knew that a large stand was to be erected on the infield for the performers. Bob and I decided that we needed several cameras in front of the bandstand, one to cover the entire action from one side of the stand to the other, and others to shoot individual shots of the performers and tight group shots as The Beatles sang and played their instruments. All of these cameras were to be in a duck-blind type of cover to keep them out of view of the audience. We needed other angles also, so we decided to place several cameras, mostly with long lenses, surrounding the infield. All these cameras were going to be connected with an expensive, state-of-the-art radio communications system, but all camera operators were also instructed about what to get and what not to get, and were told to function independently and shoot anything of interest, the unexpected and the unusual, in case the communication system failed. Bob and I, having seen the reactions of the audience during The Beatles' performances at the Ed Sullivan Theatre, both knew that some of the most interesting action might take place in the seats of the immense stadium. We decided to have cameras at strategic locations in the stands, ready to film the show and whatever might happen in the audience.

More and more meetings followed. Every consecutive meeting was larger, had more people involved and became more complicated and far-reaching than the meetings before. The photography of the show almost became secondary and seemed to get lost in the shuffle of all the other important considerations, such as safety. The security chief of the stadium and his staff, also aware of the

PHOTO BY GEORGE E. JOSEPH.

Here I am in the center of the "duck blind" (third from the left) checking a camera setup before the Beatles concert at Shea Stadium.

mass hysteria that accompanied every performance and public appearance by The Beatles, were becoming increasingly concerned over losing control over the crowd and feared a worst-case scenario, a stampede onto the field, which, in their estimation, could result in thousands injured and killed within just minutes. The stadium staff was going to request a very large contingent of New York City police for the concert, and in addition, stadium security recommended an extra 300 auxiliary cops be hired for the event. All sorts of other security arrangements were proposed and implemented. One was a triple-line police barricade surrounding the entire infield in front of the grandstand. These barricades were going to be laid out in such a manner that no one from the audience could jump over all three of them; they would have to be vaulted one at a time, by which time the police stationed in front of these barricades could stop the jumper. The fear was, as the stadium's chief of security told us over and over at these meetings, that if one person bolted and jumped from the grandstand, he or she might be followed by other hysterical kids, which could start a flood toward that area, as they put it, the same as water going toward a break in a dam. It was an inexplicable phenomenon, they pointed out, that an out-of-control crowd always converges on the point of the break and tries to squeeze through even the smallest opening. In the estimation of the security experts, a situation like this, with thousands pushing from behind, could not be effectively dealt with, and thousands could get trampled to death. This sort of thing had to be stopped within the first few seconds, before it could spread through the crowd. There were going to be ushers, guards and police at every aisle, a ring of them in the stands and a very large contingent in the field just in front of the triple barricades. But injuries, they pointed out, were unavoidable. Even without hysteria, there were always injuries during ball games — people falling, fainting, having heart attacks, choking on hot dogs and so on. A first-aid station large enough to deal with a large problem was proposed.

The more of these meeting I attended, the more I wondered why I'd decided to accept this project. Just moving around in the stands called for an armed escort for the camera crews. All were advised never to run, no matter what the urgency might be to get to another location, as even something like that could trigger people in the audience to follow and start a riot.

The enormity of my end of the job was beginning to manifest itself more and more as I got more deeply involved. The first and perhaps biggest concern I had was getting proper exposure for my cameras. The bandstand was not going to be a problem. It was, I knew, going to be brightly illuminated, and though lighting it was not altogether under my control, I had enough input to adjust the light levels for good exposure. But in turn, this created and brought home another problem, which was the photography of the audience. The higher the light levels were on the bandstand, the darker the audience in the grandstand was going to appear. The gigantic ring of lights atop the stadium were all directed and focused on the playing field, giving the audience a minimum of light, enough only to find seats, go to the toilet or see the vendors. But when I went to Shea to measure this light, it turned out to be woefully below the level I needed for good photography. Though this gave me some very anxious moments, in retrospect, even this aspect of my work turned out to be interesting.

First of all, I needed unlimited access to all parts of the stadium and the stands for my fact-finding trips. Going to the stadium on the night of a game was only partially useful, as with the game in progress, I could not go onto the field to measure the light intensities. When there was no game, the lights were off, and turning them on even for a short time cost thousands of dollars. But I needed to know, and the lights were turned on for me. Besides the need for certain light levels for exposure, I also had to be concerned with the color of the lights. My contact at the stadium told me that the original lights installed on the roof were all of a mercury-vapor variety, producing an intense, blue light. Motion-picture film is balanced for a certain color, and at that time I needed an illumination that was more red than blue. Expressed in technical terms, I needed 3400° Kelvin color-temperature lights for 3400° Kelvin-rated film. The blue light was way above this rating and would have produced very blue images. I, of course, could have corrected this with filters, but every time a filter is placed in front of a lens more light is required for exposure, and "more light" I didn't have.

Fortunately for me, additional lights were installed in the stadium, my contact told me, because the blue lights were hard on the audience's eyes. Besides, it was discovered that focusing on a fast-moving object like a baseball in the blue light presented a problem; outfielders consistently misjudged where the ball was and couldn't catch it. It became necessary to install quartz-iodine lights to help ballplayers see the ball, and much to my relief, they were of the proper color temperature for photography. But they didn't completely solve my problems — they helped with the photography of the concert but offered very little help with the photography of the audience. In 1966, color motion-picture film was not sensitive enough to photograph under low-light conditions, and I knew that unless I came up with some sort of a solution for photographing the audience, the show was not going to have a possibly very interesting element: the excitement of the audience and its reaction to what was going on onstage. A big part of "Beatlemania," the high-pitched reactions of the kids, perhaps the most interesting part of the show, might be lost because of a lack of light.

I took advantage of my free pass and unlimited access to go to ball games, taking a small camera and filming audience shots. I experimented with exposure, faster lenses and hand-held lights and turned the film over to my good friend John Kowalik at the lab. John developed and printed this footage, wringing every drop of value out of it, until we came up with a formula that was going to allow me almost unlimited opportunities to film the audience. Indeed, some of those shots — tears running down both cheeks of a teenaged girl, kids jumping up and down and more — became interesting highlights of the show.

I arrived at the stadium early on the morning of August 15, 1965, the day of the concert. By that time there was a large number of cars in the parking lot, and a never-ending chain of others was arriving. Kids were getting out of sleeping bags near the ticket windows, and some were already inside the stadium. I had an assigned parking spot in the employees' lot, close to one of the employee entrances, and had no problem getting into the stadium. Most of my crew was already there, setting up cameras and getting organized. Within a short time, under the direction of Bob Precht, we were making shots of all the activities as the finishing touches were applied to the grandstand, people were beginning to arrive, and sound systems were tested. My crew and I went over the safety procedures with one of the stadium security officers, who explained and pointed out our escape routes in case of a large-scale riot. I had four possible escape routes, depending on where I was if and when something necessitated an escape. By 2 or 3 o'clock in the afternoon, all was ready, and by about 4 o'clock the stadium seemed to be filled to capacity. But people were still coming in, and long before the lights came on, ripples of screaming tore through the stadium. Recorded music was played to entertain the audience, but the screaming was so loud at times that I couldn't hear the music, even though I was standing next to one of the 7-foot-high speakers set up 10 feet apart on the foul line.

It was almost show time. Before long, the lights came on over the bandstand and the concert started. A variety of well-known groups, Sounds Incorporated, The King Curtis Band and the Discotheque Dancers, were warming up the audience. But the audience didn't need warming up. As the large New York Airways helicopter appeared overhead and slowly descended onto the parking lot — even before the station-wagon bringing The Beatles from the parking lot reached the bandstand — the screams of an estimated 56,000 people, mostly teenaged girls and boys, filled the stadium. The electricity in the air was amazing and indescribable. So was the noise. The perfect circle that Shea Stadium is focused the earsplitting screams of the crowd onto the infield and almost totally negated the output of the large, amplified speakers. The headphones and microphone, part of the state-of-the-art communication system that linked me to the cameras, were useless. I took mine off, tossed them into the blind in front of the grandstand, and balled up an almost-full package of lens-cleaning tissue to stuff into my ears. It didn't help. The top-of-the-line, expensive earplugs that I purchased after my disastrous flight simulating jet travel were in my lightmeter case in the camera room, deep in the belly of the stadium, too far at this point to be fetched. The concert was in full swing and I couldn't leave. Surely, all of us expected loud reactions from the audience, but none of us had any idea how loud "loud" could be. And the intensity of the noise kept building. I ran desperately from camera position to camera position and, by using sign language and a note pad, communicated as well as I could with my crews. It is to their credit that the show was so thoroughly covered and turned out so well. The Beatles' music and singing could no longer be heard as the noise surpassed imagination, and the music became secondary to being in the presence of The Beatles, who, in the words of John Lennon, were more popular at that time than Jesus.

But we were all caught up in the excitement. I had a ladder stashed under the bandstand that I intended to use to get high-angle close shots whenever something looked good on the stage. I was on the top of this ladder, grinding away, when the ladder shook violently and I realized a small man was shaking it. I told him to stop, but he didn't, and in order to avoid falling I climbed down. I was about to swing at the man, who turned out to be Beatles promoter Sid Bernstein, who didn't want the ladder obstructing the view of some in the audience. But there was so much going on that I decided to go after other targets to film instead of arguing with him.

As I went from spot to spot, looking for shots in the audience, I noticed here and there kids, mostly sobbing, crying, little girls, who would stand up, start to jump rhythmically in place as though jumping rope; and a few seconds later, some would run screaming down an aisle and jump — or try to jump — into the infield. The ushers and cops would chase them, but some managed to leap over the barricades, only to be grabbed by cops who hauled them away. I photographed the entire process as one little girl vaulted over the police lines. I thought the fall would kill her, but it took four cops to control her and take her to the detention area. I thought this was going to be good "cut-in" material, but the shot didn't make the cut. The action was so violent, her struggle to get to The Beatles was so fierce, that it was decided not to include this shot in the show. Less violent but similar material was included. The "jumpers," as the police called these little girls, had to be dealt with quickly in their own interest, as well as in the interest of all in the stadium. Long before The Beatles finished, the extra-large first-aid area created especially for this event was overflowing with injured, bandaged and still-weeping kids and their terrified mothers.

But the screaming never stopped. The noise of my ride on the outside of a plane in flight appeared anemic by comparison. My head was splitting, but I really had no time to deal with it as I kept shooting roll after roll of film. This was the first really large-scale concert given by any group, and the excitement, the reaction of the audience, was incredible, impossible to describe. The concert was over in what seemed like no time at all, and before I knew it, The Beatles were whisked off the bandstand into a waiting ambulance and were heading out of the stadium to the waiting helicopter. I knew in advance that they were going to leave in an ambulance. This was one of the early suggestions made by the security people, who believed that even in a worst-case scenario, crowds would get out of the way of an ambulance with its lights flashing and siren blaring. But the noise didn't let up. Even as the helicopter circled overhead and slowly disappeared in the direction of Manhattan, the piercing screaming continued, and the audience gave no sign of wanting to leave the stadium. My crew and I kept shooting. We made shots of the helicopter overhead, and at the same time, another of my crews filmed The Beatles in the chopper and the scene in the stadium from the air. We photographed the empty bandstand, abandoned instruments, the drums without a drummer, and relieved policemen standing around wiping their foreheads — anything and everything that caught our eyes. We filmed anxious mothers trying to steer still-screaming kids to their cars somewhere amongst the thousands of cars in the parking lots, and kids who were sitting motionless, as though mesmerized, with tears still rolling down their cheeks. Then, as the lights snapped off over the bandstand, the stadium started to empty.

I went from camera position to camera position, trying to get a quick report on what each particular camera got, but I soon realized that although I saw my camera operators' lips move, I couldn't hear what they were telling me. I found out later they didn't hear me, either. I stayed in the dark stadium long after the last light went off as my crews used light from flashlights to disassemble the cameras, unload the film from the magazines and get the film ready to go to the lab. (Fourteen cameras shot close to 200,000 feet of film that night, and when the film was developed and printed, it took us several days to look at all of it. The final show was cut to two hours, a total of 10,800 feet of film, roughly 5 percent of what we shot.)

Bob and I shook hands with a sigh of relief. It was a wrap. Bob's wife, Betty, and their children joined us on the infield, but I couldn't talk with them, either. To say that my ears were buzzing would be the understatement of the century. The noise inside my head, I imagined, could have been compared to standing between two fighter jets with their engines at full throttle, afterburners pointing directly at my ears. The pain was excruciating. I have no recollection of my trip home, a less-than-30-mile drive from Shea Stadium. What I do recall is the unbearable pain in my ears that kept me from falling asleep that night and continued for days afterward.

A week or so later, as the pain abated somewhat, I noticed that the sounds and noises around me were very different. My wife and children's voices were strange, and when I talked, my own voice sounded like somebody else was saying the words from a distance, speaking from inside a large, metal drum. My hearing has not been the same since; it has never fully gone back to what it was before The Beatles, and I don't expect it ever will. I walk around with hearing aids in both ears nowadays, but even with them, I have difficulty hearing some sounds. I have worked with several other rock groups since, including John Lennon after The Beatles broke up, at his concert in Madison Square Garden in New York. None of these concerts, as good as some were, even came close to the excitement and the extraordinary experience of filming the granddaddy of all rock concerts, *The Beatles Live at Shea Stadium*.

And nothing ever will!

EPILOGUE

The piercing screams of thousands of hysterical kids, the noise of the crowd in Shea Stadium that would have made thunder pale with envy, still ring in my ears. The pain that penetrated my brain abated long ago and, pain and all, I look back on that experience with pride, knowing that I was part of "being there." Being part of history, as in the case of meeting and photographing Fidel Castro, would not have happened without the business that was so kind to me and afforded such unusual and great opportunities. Recalling these experiences, or the possibility that I might have been the "first civilized person" in a remote, uncharted corner of the world, still brings on a smile and fills me with satisfaction. As the many memories flood back, I realize that the preceding chapters represent but a fraction, the virtual tip of the iceberg of thousands of unusual and memorable experiences that happened during the course of more than half a century of film-making.

During that time, I often heard "It's a wrap," at times signaling the end of an arduous day, and at other times announcing that some-thing unexpected, disastrous or funny had stopped us in our tracks. When, during a rehearsal, Sylvester Stallone, in a macho moment, threw a stuntman through an expensive breakaway window, the only one we had, which, due to its immense size and extremely delicate nature, had to be specially crated and brought to our British Columbia location, it was definitely one of those occasions when "It's a wrap" was quietly on the lips of more than a few of our crew people. At that moment, "It's a wrap" not only signaled a costly and catastrophic moment in the production, one that shut us down, but it also offered an unsaid yet eloquent comment on the situation. And when tons of our "garbage" disappeared, taken away by the New York Department of

Sanitation, nothing could have better stated our situation than "It's a wrap."

Looking back on those years, I cannot help but recall fondly some of the great experiences. I smile as they come to mind; laugh out loud at some of the funny ones, even if it involved the sinking of a borrowed, million-dollar powerboat; or recoil with horror, remembering incidents like real cops about to shoot an actor, believing that the actor was a criminal shooting at the police.

Almost all film projects, certainly the ones I was involved in, had their share of unusual and, in most cases, unanticipated incidents, or offered fantastic opportunities to see places and do things that I would never have had the opportunity to experience without the movie business. How many people can travel the world, lay claim to capsizing in a camera boat in the raging rapids of an uncharted region in the South American rainforest, or ride into the dusk of an Arctic afternoon toward Siberia in a dogsled? Meeting, working with and getting to know the headline-makers, famous and interesting people of all walks of life, makes me look back on those years with fondness and remember some days when I wished that the announcement signaling the end of the workday, "It's a wrap," would never come. On the other hand, under the pressures of a production, when even the trivial seemed devastatingly larger than life, when hearing "It's a wrap" was fervently hoped for, it would almost never come soon enough. But film projects always ended, wrapping too quickly at times or dragging on and on and on. Yet even the ones that tested my sanity have been transformed by the passing of time, the great healer, banishing all that was bad to oblivion and allowing only the good moments to be remembered. And there were always new projects to look forward to, ones that would be even better than the last, with unique opportunities and promises, and surprises to be added to the list of disasters that happened on films that wrapped long ago.

The stories are endless. I hope that the few in this book have been of interest to you, bringing you closer to the inner workings of filmmaking and offering a look in on the day-to-day lives and activities of filmmakers during production.

Whatever the case, for now, this book is a wrap!

ACKNOWLEDGEMENTS

If I were an architect or knew exactly what kind of house I would like to build, even if I could draw up the most precise, elaborate plans, I would still need the help of those who truly how my plans could be executed. The layman's sketches or the architect's drawings, as well defined and detailed as they might be, are a long way from opening the front door and walking into the finished structure.

In some ways, bringing a book to publication is very similar to and possibly even more demanding than building a house. One can always add a room, put on a second floor or repaint a wall if the color is not exactly right. But before a book goes to press, one must be absolutely certain about whether all the commas are in the right place, whether a word should be capitalized or lowercase or have quotation marks or brackets, and whether the period should be inside or outside the parenthesis.

And what should the book look like? How big, small or thick should it be? What should be on the cover? What kind of paper should it be printed on and what sort of typeface should be used? The questions are endless, and the answers, the meticulous care given to all the painstaking detail, are demanding and time-consuming.

It would not be possible to give credit to all those who play a part in bringing a book to the shelf in the bookstore, but credit must be given to those who played a major part in turning an author's work into reality. For this book, the first such credit must go to my wife, who put up with me as I pounded the keyboard from morning till night, shirking the share of household chores that should have been mine. And when the last period was placed after the last word of the last sentence of the "perfect" book, she took the book with a smile and started making red marks in the text and notes in the margin. It was almost irritating to have her tell me that my tenses were out of kilter, or ask questions about things that were crystal-clear to me and tell me that a reader who wasn't as familiar with the subject matter would have difficulty relating to what I thought was obvious. But her work immeasurably improved what I put on paper, as she stuck to her guns even in the face of my fierce insistence that my material, as I'd written it, was better. The work of the professionals who followed her proved her right.

The first of these, Rachael Bosley, it seemed gave up her youth, devoting all her time to working on this book. Her tireless and, I should say, relentless work — her patient explanations as to why a sentence should be restructured, and why some material, as dear as it was to me, should be cut because the same sentence, almost word for word, was on the previous page — was a very convincing illustration of the importance of her attention and expertise.

When the text was finally correct, with commas, periods, quotation marks and parentheses in place, the work of taking the pages and turning them into a book started. How many fledgling authors ever noticed that a new chapter always starts on the right-hand page? Or that the table of contents, foreword and introduction have to be in a certain order? Or that photographs and illustrations have to be in their proper places, and the page numbers must correlate with the page numbers next to the names of people, places and things in the index? And what should the cover design be? What should go on the back cover of the book? This is but the tip of the iceberg! My gratitude goes out to Martha Winterhalter, who didn't let the slightest detail escape her in formatting, structuring and publishing this volume.

No amount of "thank-yous" could adequately express my gratitude to Martha and Rachael!

I also want to express my appreciation to the many friends who, having heard some of my stories, thought that I should compile them in a book. Film students and film professionals who listened to my "war stories" felt that they could learn from my experiences, even if those experiences were disastrous, and also strongly recommended I publish a collection of them.

Thank you all for your encouragement and support!

Gratefully,
Andrew Laszlo
April 2004

FILMOGRAPHY

FILM AND TELEVISION

1992   *Newsies*
Walt Disney Pictures

1990   *Ghost Dad*
Universal Pictures

1989   *Star Trek V:*
The Final Frontier
Paramount Pictures

1987   *Innerspace*
Amblin Entertainment-
Warner Bros.

1986   *Poltergeist II*
MGM

1985   *Remo Williams:*
The Adventure Begins
Orion Pictures

1984   *Thief of Hearts*
Paramount Pictures

1983   *Streets of Fire*
Universal Pictures

Love Is Forever
20th Century Fox

1982   *First Blood*
Carolco-Orion Pictures

I, The Jury
20th Century Fox

1981   *Southern Comfort*
20th Century Fox

1980   *The Funhouse*
Universal Pictures

Shōgun
Paramount Television

Thin Ice
CBS

1979   *The Warriors*
Paramount Pictures

Somebody Killed
Her Husband
Columbia Pictures

Angela
Zev Braun Productions

Top of the Hill
Paramount Television

1978   *The Dain Curse*
CBS/Martin Poll
Productions

Spanner's Key
Paramount Television

1977   *Thieves*
Paramount Pictures

1977	*Washington: Behind Closed Doors* Paramount Television	1966	*You're A Big Boy Now* Seven Arts Productions

1977   *Washington: Behind Closed Doors*
Paramount Television

1976   *Countdown at Kusini*
Independent

1974   *The Unwanted*
John Secondary Productions

1973   *Class of '44*
Warner Bros.

1972   *To Find A Man*
Columbia Pictures

The Man Without A Country
Norman Rosemont Productions

1971   *Jennifer on My Mind*
United Artists

1970   *The Owl and the Pussycat*
Columbia Pictures

Lovers and Other Strangers
ABC Films/Cinerama

The Out of Towners
Paramount Pictures

The Ed Sullivan Vietnam Veterans Easter Special
CBS

1969   *Popi*
United Artists

Blue Water Gold
Metromedia Productions

1968   *The Night They Raided Minsky's*
United Artists

1967   *Teacher, Teacher*
Hallmark Hall of Fame

1966   *You're A Big Boy Now*
Seven Arts Productions

Daphne
CBS

The Beatles at Shea Stadium
Ed Sullivan Productions/ABC

1965   *The Cliffdwellers*
Bing Crosby Productions

The Happeners
Plautus Productions

1964   *One Potato, Two Potato*
Independent

Coronet Blue
Plautus Productions

The Doctors and the Nurses
Plautus Productions

1962   *The Nurses*
Plautus Productions

1959-63   *Naked City*
Columbia Pictures/
Screen Gems

1960   *The Twentieth Century*
CBS

1959   *Ed Sullivan in Cuba*
CBS

1958   *High Adventure with Lowell Thomas*
Odyssey Productions/CBS

Brenner
CBS

1953-57   *The Phil Silvers Show*
CBS

Ed Sullivan in Ireland
CBS

| 1953–57 | *Ed Sullivan in Alaska*
CBS | 1954 | *Mama*
CBS |
| | *Ed Sullivan in Portugal*
CBS | 1953 | *Joe and Mabel*
CBS |

≈ ≈ ≈ ≈ ≈

COMMERCIALS

"Glass Act"
U.S. Sprint

"Buck Williams"
Sports Illustrated

"Vacation"
American Express

"Alley"
Pontiac

"Alumni"
Miller Light Beer

"Fireman's Fund"
IBM

"Jockey"
Sports Illustrated

"First Date"
American Express

"Stuck Sleigh"
Kroger

"Heartbeat"
Chevrolet

"Bonneville"
Pontiac

"Men in Booth"
OTB

"Screen"
Dyfonate

"Famous Dogs"
Stroh's Beer

"Again and Again"
Toyota

"Waterfall"
Coor's Beer

"Florida State Lottery"
(Many spots)

"Talk Radio"
"Shrink"
Publisher's Clearing
House

"Palmer/American
Garage"
"Palmer/Gas Station"
"Palmer/Latrobe C.C."
Pennzoil

"Power Trip"
"Moving Office"
"One On Top"
"Business Is Up"
Cellular One

"Father and Son"
Oldsmobile

"Are We There Yet"
Milton Bradley Toys

"ZEEMA"
Sanyo

"Nascar"
Pennzoil

"Mr. Goodwrench"
"Spring Break"
GM

"Kenny Bernstein"
Budweiser

"Vampire"
"Bad Lands"
Pontiac

"Spoke Person"
"Big Shoulders"
Head and Shoulders
- Proctor and
Gamble

"Number One"
Jiffy Lube -
Arnold Palmer

"Problems/Solutions"
Gumouts

≈ ≈ ≈ ≈ ≈

PROFESSIONAL MEMBERSHIPS

American Society of Cinematographers

International Cinematographers Guild,
Hollywood and New York

Directors Guild of America

Academy of Motion Picture Arts and Sciences

Academy of Television Arts and Sciences

INDEX